More
ENCOUNTERS

15 More Stirring Tales and Exciting Encounters
With Reading, Comprehension, Literature, and Writing SKILLS

by Burton Goodman

Glencoe
McGraw-Hill

New York, New York   Columbus, Ohio   Chicago, Illinois   Peoria, Illinois   Woodland Hills, California

JAMESTOWN  EDUCATION

TITLES IN THE SERIES

Adventures	Level B	After Shocks	Level E
More Adventures	Level B	Sudden Twists	Level F
Chills	Level C	More Twists	Level F
More Chills	Level C	Encounters	Level G
Surprises	Level D	More Encounters	Level G
More Surprises	Level D	Conflicts	Level H
Shocks	Level E	More Conflicts	Level H

Glencoe/McGraw-Hill

A Division of The McGraw-Hill Companies

More Encounters

Cover and text design: Patricia Volpe, adapted from the original
   design by Deborah Hulsey Christie
Cover illustration: Bob Eggleton
Text illustrations:
Jan Naimo Jones: pp. 45, 119
Pamela R. Levy: pp. 36–37
David Opie: pp. 8–9, 127
Lance Paladino: pp. 76–77, 93
Marcy Ramsey: pp. 26, 63, 103
Joel Synder: pp. 19, 87
Adam Young: pp. 52–53, 69, 110–111

ISBN : 0-89061-769-4

Send all Inquiries to:
Glencoe/McGraw-Hill
8787 Orion Place
Columbus, OH 43240

10 11 12 13 14 116 / 055 09 08 07 06 05

Contents

To the Student   5

The Short Story—Literary Terms   7

1. The Legend of Sleepy Hollow *by Washington Irving*   8

2. The Wise and the Weak *by Philip Aponte*   19

3. Dear Marsha *by Judie Angell*   26

4. Polar Night *by Norah Burke*   36

5. I'll Give You Law *by Molly Picon*   45

6. A Habit for the Voyage *by Robert Edmond Alter*   52

7. Eleven *by Sandra Cisneros*   63

8. The Clearing *by Jesse Stuart*   69

9. The Medicine Bag *by Virginia Driving Hawk Sneve*   76

10. The Fun They Had *by Isaac Asimov*   87

11. Lonesome Boy *by Arna Bontemps*   93

12. My Father Goes to Court *by Carlos Bulosan*   103

13. The Piece of String *by Guy de Maupassant*   110

14. Finding the Way *by Helen Keller*   119

15. The Town Where No One Got Off *by Ray Bradbury*   127

Acknowledgments   134

Progress Chart   135

Progress Graph   136

To the Student

This book contains 15 outstanding stories, each of recognized literary value. Within these pages you will find time-honored authors, as well as present-day writers. You will find, too, that many countries and cultures are represented.

As the title suggests, each selection in this volume involves an encounter. There are, of course, many different kinds of encounters. As you might expect, there are encounters with enemies and danger. But characters also look within themselves, as they encounter questions dealing with personal courage and conscience. All of these, and more, are presented here.

These stories will provide you with many hours of reading pleasure, and the exercises that follow offer a wide variety of ways to help you improve your reading and literature skills. In fact, the exercises have been specially designed with *skill* mastery in mind:

SELECTING DETAILS FROM THE STORY

KNOWING NEW VOCABULARY WORDS

IDENTIFYING STORY ELEMENTS

LOOKING AT CLOZE

LEARNING HOW TO READ CRITICALLY

SELECTING DETAILS FROM THE STORY will help you improve your reading comprehension skills.

KNOWING NEW VOCABULARY WORDS will help you strengthen your vocabulary skills. Often, you will be able to figure out the meaning of an unfamiliar word by using *context clues*—the words and phrases around the word.

IDENTIFYING STORY ELEMENTS will give you practice in recognizing and understanding the key elements of literature.

LOOKING AT CLOZE will help you reinforce your reading *and* your vocabulary skills through the use of the cloze technique.

LEARNING HOW TO READ CRITICALLY will help you sharpen your critical thinking skills. You will have opportunities to *reason* by drawing conclusions, making inferences, using story clues, and so forth.

There are four questions in each of these exercises. Do all the exercises. Then check your answers with your teacher. Use the scoring chart following each exercise to calculate your score for that exercise. Give yourself 5 points for each correct answer.

Since there are four questions, you can receive up to 20 points for each exercise. Use the SKILL scoring chart at the end of the exercises to figure your total score. A perfect score for the exercises would equal 100 points. Keep track of how well you do by recording your score on the Progress Chart on page 135. Then record your score on the Progress Graph on page 136 to plot your progress.

Another section, **Improving Writing and Discussion Skills**, offers further opportunities for thoughtful discussion and creative writing.

On the following page, you will find brief definitions of some important literary terms. If you wish, refer to these definitions when you answer the questions in the section Identifying Story Elements.

I feel certain that you will enjoy reading the stories in this book. And the exercises that follow will help you master a number of very important skills.

Now . . . get ready for some *More Encounters!*

Burton Goodman

The Short Story—Literary Terms

Character Development: the change in a character from the beginning to the conclusion of the story.

Characterization: the ways a writer shows what a character is like. The way a character acts, speaks, thinks, and looks *characterizes* that person.

Climax: the turning point of a story.

Conflict: a struggle or difference of opinion between characters. Sometimes a character may clash with a force of nature.

Dialogue: the exact words that a character says; usually the conversation between characters.

Foreshadowing: clues that hint or suggest what will happen later in the story.

Inner Conflict: a struggle that takes place in the mind of a character.

Main Character: the person the story is mostly about.

Mood: the feeling or atmosphere that the writer creates. For example, the *mood* of a story might be humorous or suspenseful.

Motive: the reason behind a character's actions.

Narrator: the person who tells the story. Usually, the *narrator* is the writer or a character in the story.

Plot: the series of incidents or happenings in a story. The *plot* is the outline or arrangement of events.

Purpose: the reason the author wrote the story. For example, an author's *purpose* might be to amuse or entertain, to convince, or to inform.

Setting: the time and place of the action in a story; where and when the action takes place.

Style: the way in which a writer uses language. The choice and arrangement of words and sentences help to create the writer's *style*.

Theme: the main, or central idea, of a story.

I. The Legend of Sleepy Hollow

by Washington Irving

Meet the Author

Washington Irving (1783–1859) was the first American writer to gain worldwide fame. Born in New York City at the beginning of the Revolutionary War, he was named after George Washington. Irving's works include short stories and essays, biographies, and books about Spanish history and culture. His two most popular stories, "The Legend of Sleepy Hollow," and "Rip Van Winkle" appear in *The Sketch Book*.

*I*n one of those spacious coves along the eastern shore of the Hudson River lies a small village, which is known by the name of Tarrytown. About two miles from this village, there is a little valley hidden among high hills. It is one of the quietest places in the whole world. A small brook glides through it, whose murmur is just enough to lull one to sleep. The occasional whistling of a quail, or tapping of a woodpecker, is almost the only sound that ever breaks in upon its silence.

Because of the peaceful nature of the place and the drowsy character of its inhabitants, this valley has long been known by the name of Sleepy Hollow. A dreamy cloud seems to hang over the land. Some say that the place was put under a spell many years ago, before the area was explored by Henry Hudson. Certainly, the people there are given to all kinds of strange beliefs. They frequently see visions and hear voices in the air. The whole neighborhood abounds with tales of haunted spots and ghosts and goblins.

The main spirit that haunts this region is a figure on horseback without a head. It is said to be the ghost of a Hessian[1] soldier, whose head had been knocked off by a cannonball during the Revolutionary War. He is frequently seen hurrying along in the gloom of night, as if riding on the wings of the wind. Some claim that the ghost rides forth in search of his head. And he is known to one and all as the Headless Horseman of Sleepy Hollow.

In this place there lived some years ago, a man by the name of Ichabod Crane, who settled in Sleepy Hollow to teach the children of the vicinity.

The name *Crane* was appropriate to his person. He was tall, but extremely thin, with narrow shoulders and long arms and legs. His hands dangled a mile out of his sleeves, and his feet might have served for shovels. His whole frame, in fact, was very loosely hung together. His head was small and flat at the top, with huge ears, large green glassy eyes, and a long, sharp nose. To see him striding along on a windy day, with his clothes flapping and fluttering about him, one might have mistaken him for a scarecrow escaped from a cornfield.

Ichabod's log schoolhouse consisted of one large room. It stood in a lonely but pleasant spot, at the foot of a hill near a brook. The low murmur of his pupils repeating their lessons might be heard, like the hum of bees on a drowsy summer day. Now and then the voice of the master interrupted, in a tone of menace or command, as he urged some pupil along the road of knowledge. Truth to tell, he was a conscientious man who always kept in mind the following words: "Spare the rod and spoil the child." Ichabod's students certainly were not spoiled!

When school hours were over, Ichabod was the friend and companion of the older boys. And on holiday afternoons he would accompany home some of the younger boys— especially those whose mothers were known for their excellent cooking. Indeed, he had no choice but to stay on good terms with his pupils, for while his income was small, his appetite was enormous.

As was the custom in those parts, he lived for a week at a time at the houses of the farmers whose children he instructed. Thus every week he made the rounds of the neighborhood with all his worldly goods tied up in a cotton handkerchief. In return, he occasionally assisted the farmers in the lighter labors of the farm. He was also the singing teacher of the neighborhood, by which he earned a little extra money. As a result he just managed to get by, although those who didn't know better thought that he lived a wonderfully easy life.

Ichabod was considered to be a man of great learning, for he had read several books from beginning to end. He was an expert on Cotton Mather's *History of New England Witchcraft*, a book in which he most firmly believed.

It was often Ichabod's pleasure after school was dismissed, to stretch out near the little brook by the schoolhouse. There he would read old Mather's frightening tales until the dusk of evening made it difficult to see. Then, as he made his way back to the farmhouse

---

1. **Hessian:** A German soldier hired by the British to fight the Americans during the Revolutionary War.

where he happened to be staying that week, every sound terrified his excited imagination—perhaps to drive evil spirits away. The good people of Sleepy Hollow were often filled with awe on hearing his high, piping voice floating down from the distant hills.

Another of his fearful pleasures was to pass long winter evenings with the old Dutch wives, as they sat spinning wool by the fire. Then he would listen to their tales of ghosts and goblins and haunted woods and haunted bridges and haunted houses, and particularly of the Headless Horseman of Sleepy Hollow. Ichabod, in turn, would delight them with his own tales of witchcraft and amazing stories of comets and shooting stars.

But though he took pleasure in this, sitting in a snug room near a crackling fireplace, he paid for it dearly when he walked home later. What horrible shapes and shadows crossed his path in the ghastly glare of a snowy night! How often was he terrified by the sound of his very own steps! And how often did he shake with dread at the roar of the wind howling through the trees— afraid that it was the Headless Horseman on one of his nightly rides!

Among those who assembled one evening each week to receive singing lessons was Katrina Van Tassel. She was the only child of a wealthy Dutch farmer. She was a lass of eighteen, rosy-cheeked, and famous for her beauty. She was also known as a bit of a flirt.

Ichabod had a soft and foolish heart toward the ladies. No wonder then that Katrina soon found favor in his eyes— especially after he had visited her in her magnificent mansion. Old Baltus Van Tassel was the very picture of a thriving and prosperous farmer. His home was situated on one of the prettiest spots on the banks of the Hudson. Close to his spacious farmhouse was a vast barn that contained turkeys, pigeons, pigs, and geese, and every treasure of the farm.

The teacher's mouth watered as, in his mind's eye, he saw future meals. He saw roast pigs, each with an apple in its mouth. He pictured pigeons in pigeon pie, geese swimming in their own gravy, ducks dipped in onion sauce, and turkeys draped with sausages. The enraptured Ichabod imagined all of this. And—as he rolled his large green eyes over the rolling meadowlands—he beheld fields of wheat, of rye, of corn, and an orchard overflowing with fruit—and his heart yearned for Katrina who would inherit these riches.

When he entered the house, Ichabod's heart was completely won over. Everywhere fine furniture sparkled. Dark mahogany tables shone like mirrors, and a corner cupboard displayed treasures of old silver and valuable china.

From that moment on, Ichabod's main concern was how to gain the affections of the wonderful daughter of Baltus Van Tassel. In this matter, however, he faced obstacles, for she had many admirers.

Among these, the most formidable was a rough and burly, fun-loving young fellow who went by the name of Brom Van Brunt. Brom was the hero of the countryside because of his feats of courage and strength. He was broad-shouldered and rugged, with short, curly black hair. Because of his mighty frame and tremendous powers of limb, he had been given the nickname, "Brom Bones." Brom was famous for his skill in horsemanship and was always ready for a fight, though there was more mischief than ill will in his nature.

He had three or four good friends who considered him their leader. Sometimes his crew could be heard dashing past the farmhouses in the dead of night. Then the neighbors, startled out of their sleep, would exclaim, "There goes Brom Bones and his gang!" He was looked upon with a mixture of awe, admiration, and goodwill, and when any prank or brawl occurred in the neighborhood, people shook their heads and guessed that Brom Bones was at the bottom of it. Such was the rival with whom Ichabod had to deal!

Under cover of his role as singing teacher, Ichabod made frequent visits to the Van Tassel farmhouse. Meanwhile, Ichabod became the object of many practical jokes by Brom Bones and his gang. They smoked out his singing school by stopping up the chimney. They continually broke into the schoolhouse at night and turned everything upside down, until the poor schoolmaster began to think that all the witches in the country held their meetings there. But what was most annoying, Brom took every opportunity to make Ichabod look foolish to Katrina. For example, Brom taught an old dog to whine in the most ridiculous manner, then introduced it to Katrina as a rival singing teacher. Matters went on in this way for some time.

One fine afternoon Ichabod sat on his high stool in his classroom from where he looked down on his students. His scholars were all busily reading their books—or slyly whispering behind them with one eye on the master. A kind of buzzing stillness filled the classroom. It was suddenly interrupted by the appearance of a messenger. He came clattering up to the school door with an invitation to attend a dance at Mister Van Tassel's house that evening.

All was now hustle and bustle in the late afternoon schoolroom. The scholars were quickly hurried through their lessons. Books were flung aside without being put away on the shelves, benches were thrown down, and the whole school was let out an hour before the usual time.

Ichabod now spent at least an extra half an hour brushing his best and only suit of rusty black. He carefully arranged his hair, using as a mirror a piece of broken glass that he found in the schoolhouse.

To arrive in style, he borrowed a horse from the farmer with whom he was currently lodged, an old Dutchman by the name of Hans Van Ripper. Thus, gallantly mounted, Ichabod rode forth like a knight in search of adventure.

The animal he set out on was actually a broken-down plow horse that had outlived almost everything but its viciousness. It was gaunt and shaggy, with a thin neck and a head like a hammer. One eye had lost its pupil and was glaring, while the other had a terrible gleam in it. Still, he must have been fiery and spirited in his day, if we may judge from the name it was given—"Gunpowder."

Ichabod was a suitable figure for such a horse. He rode with short stirrups, which brought his knees nearly up to the saddle. His sharp elbows stuck out like grasshoppers, and as his horse jogged on, the motion of Ichabod's arms was like the flapping of a pair of wings. A small woolen hat rested on the top of Ichabod's head, and the back of his black coat fluttered out almost to the horse's tail. Ichabod and his horse were a sight such as is seldom seen in broad daylight!

It was toward evening that Ichabod arrived at the Van Tassel mansion. Farmers and their wives, sons and daughters, dressed in their fashionable best, had already arrived. Brom Bones, however, was the hero of the scene, having come to the gathering on his favorite horse, Daredevil, a creature like himself, high-spirited and full of mischief.

Ichabod entered and gazed with rapture upon the display of heaped-up platters of food. There were cakes of every kind and description—sweet cakes, short cakes, ginger cakes, and honey cakes. And there were pies—apple pies, peach pies, and pumpkin pies. There were slices of ham and smoked beef, and there were dishes of plums, peaches, and pears; not to mention broiled fish and roasted chickens. Ichabod could not help rolling his large eyes around him as he ate, and chuckling over the possibility that he might, one day, be lord of all this marvelous luxury and splendor. *Then,* thought he, he'd turn his back on the schoolhouse, snap his fingers in the face of Hans Van Ripper, and kick out any teacher who dared to call him comrade.

And now the sound of music summoned them to dance. Ichabod prided himself on his dancing—as much as on his singing. Not a limb, not a particle of him was idle, as he clattered about the room in full motion. And why should he not be joyous? For Katrina, the lady of his heart was his partner and smiled at him graciously, while Brom Bones sat in the corner, jealously brooding.

When the dance was over, Ichabod joined a group of folks who told wild and wonderful tales of ghosts and spirits and haunted places. Most of the stories, however, centered on the villagers' favorite phantom—the Headless Horseman of Sleepy Hollow. He had been seen, it seems, several times of late, patrolling the countryside.

Brom Bones, in fact, declared that on returning one night from a neighboring village, he had been approached by the midnight rider. Bones had offered to race him for a bowl of punch—and would have won it too, said Bones—for Daredevil was beating the ghost's horse easily. But just as they came to the church bridge, the Headless Horseman bolted away and vanished in a flash of fire!

All these tales sank deep in the mind of Ichabod Crane.

The party now gradually broke up. The farmers gathered together their families and started for home. Ichabod, convinced that he was on the road to success, lingered behind to speak privately with Katrina. What was said, we do not know. Something, however, must have gone very wrong!—for he suddenly rushed out, keenly disappointed. Without looking to the right or the left, he went straight to the stable, got on his horse, and departed.

It was the very witching time of night. The hour was as dismal as himself. In the dead hush of midnight, he could hear the barking of a watchdog on the other side of the Hudson. All the stories of ghosts and goblins that he had heard earlier now came rushing back into his memory. The night grew darker and darker; the stars seemed to sink deeper in the sky. He had never felt so lonely and downcast. He was, furthermore, approaching the very spot where many of the scenes of the ghost stories had taken place.

In the center of the road stood an enormous tree. It towered like a giant above all the other trees in the neighborhood and was a kind of landmark. Its limbs were huge and gnarled.

As Ichabod approached this fearful tree, he began to whistle. He thought he heard someone, or something, whistling back— but it was only the wind sweeping through the branches. Suddenly he heard a groan— his teeth chattered and his knees banged against the saddle. But it was just one limb knocking against another in the wind. He passed the tree in safety, but new perils lay before him.

About two hundred yards from the tree, a small brook crossed the road. A few rough logs, placed side by side, served as a bridge over the stream. To pass over this bridge was the severest test. It had long been considered a haunted stream, one dangerous to cross alone after dark.

As he approached the stream, Ichabod's heart began to thump. He summoned up courage, and giving his horse several kicks in the ribs, attempted to dash briskly over the bridge. But rather than rushing forward, the stubborn animal ran to the other side of the road and plunged into some bushes. The schoolmaster gave the horse another sharp kick. At this, Gunpowder trotted, snorting, to the side of the bridge, then reared up with a suddenness that nearly sent Ichabod sprawling.

Just at that moment, a sound near the bridge caught Ichabod's ear. He saw, in the dark, at the edge of the brook, something huge, dark, and towering. It did not move but seemed gathered up in the gloom, like some gigantic monster ready to spring.

The hair of the terrified teacher rose upon his head in terror. What could he do? It was now too late to turn and flee. Besides, what chance was there of escaping the ghost, if

such it was, which could ride upon the wings of the wind? Trying to make a show of courage, Ichabod, in a shaking voice demanded, "Who are you?" Ichabod received no reply. He repeated his question in a still more frightened voice. Still, there was no answer. He closed his eyes and burst into song.

Just then a shadowy object moved, and, with a bound, stood in the middle of the road. He appeared to be a large horseman mounted on a black horse of powerful frame. The rider kept to the side of the road, jogging next to Gunpowder, who had got over his fright.

Ichabod now urged his horse on, in the hope of leaving the other behind. The stranger, however, kept pace. Ichabod's heart began to sink. He tried to sing—but his tongue stuck to the roof of his mouth. Then, at the top of a hill, Ichabod turned around and saw, outlined against the sky, the figure of the other rider—gigantic in height and wrapped in a cloak. Ichabod was horror-struck upon seeing that the figure was—*headless!* Ichabod's terror increased when he observed that the head, which should have rested on his shoulders, *was being carried along on the saddle!*

Ichabod's terror rose to desperation. He rained a shower of kicks and blows upon Gunpowder, hoping to give the other rider the slip—but the ghost galloped along with him. Away they dashed through thick and thin, stones flying, sparks flashing at every bound. Ichabod's saddle now began to give way, and he felt it slipping from him. He had just time to save himself by clutching old Gunpowder around the neck. The saddle fell to the earth, and he heard it trampled by his pursuer.

But an opening in the tree now cheered Ichabod on, for the church bridge was close at hand. "If I can just reach that bridge," thought Ichabod, "I am safe."

Just then he heard the black horse closing in behind him. He even thought that he felt his hot breath. Another sharp kick, and old Gunpowder sprang upon the bridge and thundered over the planks to the other side. Now Ichabod cast a look behind him to see if the figure would vanish—as the old tales said—in a flash of fire.

Just then he saw the ghost rise up in his saddle, rear back, and hurl his head at him! Ichabod tried to dodge the horrible missile— but too late. It struck his head with a tremendous crash, and he went tumbling headlong into the dust. The black horse and the ghost rider passed by him like a whirlwind.

The next morning the old horse was found without his saddle. Ichabod did not make his appearance at breakfast. Dinner hour came, but no Ichabod. The children waited at the schoolhouse and strolled idly about the banks of the brook, but no schoolmaster.

Hans Van Ripper now began to feel uneasy about the fate of poor Ichabod—and about his saddle. An investigation was begun and they came upon his traces. On one part of the road leading to the church, the saddle was found trampled in the dirt. The tracks of horses' hoofs, evidently at a furious pace, were traced to the bridge. Beyond this, on the bank of a brook where the water ran deep, was found the hat of the unfortunate Ichabod. And next to it—a shattered pumpkin!

The brook was searched, but the body of the schoolmaster was not to be discovered. It was finally decided that he had been carried off by the Headless Horseman.

A farmer, on returning from a visit several years later, brought home word that Ichabod Crane was still alive; that he had left the neighborhood in fear of the ghost, and because he had been dismissed by Katrina.

Brom Bones, who married Katrina shortly after his rival's disappearance, always looked very knowingly whenever the story of Ichabod was told. And he always burst into a hearty laugh at the mention of the pumpkin. This led some people to suspect that he knew more about the matter than he chose to tell.

The people of the neighborhood, however, maintain to this day that Ichabod was carried away by the ghost. It is a favorite story often told around a winter's fire. The schoolhouse, being deserted, soon fell into decay, and is said to be haunted by the spirit of the unfortunate schoolmaster. Now and then, on a late summer night, a wanderer hears his sad song echoing through the peace and quiet of Sleepy Hollow.

SELECTING DETAILS FROM THE STORY.

The following questions help you check your reading comprehension. Put an *x* in the box next to each correct answer.

1. Ichabod Crane came to Sleepy Hollow to
   - ☐ a. swap tales about ghosts and goblins.
   - ☐ b. assist the farmers in some of their chores.
   - ☐ c. teach the children of the vicinity.

2. Ichabod was interested in Katrina Van Tassel because she
   - ☐ a. was the only child of a very wealthy farmer.
   - ☐ b. showed talent as a singer.
   - ☐ c. was so modest, quiet, and shy.

3. Brom Bones took great pleasure in
   - ☐ a. reading books as he stretched out near the little brook.
   - ☐ b. playing practical jokes on Ichabod.
   - ☐ c. spending quiet evenings relaxing at home.

4. At the end of the story, Ichabod was
   - ☐ a. drowned in the brook.
   - ☐ b. struck in the head by an object that was hurled at him.
   - ☐ c. able to hide from the figure who was chasing him.

DO NOT WRITE IN THIS BOOK

KNOWING NEW VOCABULARY WORDS.

The following questions check your vocabulary skills. Put an *x* in the box next to each correct answer.

1. The murmur of the brook was just loud enough to lull one to sleep. As used here, the word *lull* means
   - ☐ a. soothe.
   - ☐ b. startle.
   - ☐ c. control.

2. Of all the obstacles Ichabod faced, the mighty Brom Bones was the most formidable. Which of the following best defines the word *formidable*?
   - ☐ a. friendly; very helpful
   - ☐ b. dreaded; difficult to overcome
   - ☐ c. satisfied; easily pleased

3. When Ichabod entered the Van Tassel mansion, he gazed with rapture at the display of heaped-up platters of food. What is the meaning of the word *rapture*?
   - ☐ a. great anger
   - ☐ b. great sorrow
   - ☐ c. great joy

4. The people of Sleepy Hollow frequently see visions and hear ghosts; the whole neighborhood abounds with tales of haunted places. Define the word *abounds*.
   - ☐ a. requires
   - ☐ b. overflows
   - ☐ c. empties

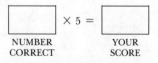

☐ × 5 = ☐

NUMBER CORRECT   YOUR SCORE

☐ × 5 = ☐

NUMBER CORRECT   YOUR SCORE

IDENTIFYING STORY ELEMENTS. The following questions check your knowledge of story elements. Put an *x* in the box next to each correct answer.

1. "The Legend of Sleepy Hollow" is *set* in a
   - ☐ a. large city.
   - ☐ b. busy town.
   - ☐ c. peaceful little valley.

2. Which sentence best *characterizes* Ichabod Crane?
   - ☐ a. He was broad-shouldered and rugged, with short, curly black hair.
   - ☐ b. He was tall and thin, with long arms and legs.
   - ☐ c. He was short and plump, with large green eyes.

3. What happened last in the *plot* of the story?
   - ☐ a. A messenger brought Ichabod an invitation to a dance at the Van Tassel home.
   - ☐ b. Ichabod tumbled into the dust and the ghost rider passed by him.
   - ☐ c. Brom Bones told of a race he had with the Headless Horseman.

4. In "The Legend of Sleepy Hollow," there is *conflict* between
   - ☐ a. Ichabod Crane and Brom Bones.
   - ☐ b. Brom Bones and Katrina Van Tassel.
   - ☐ c. Ichabod Crane and Baltus Van Tassel.

LOOKING AT CLOZE. The following questions use the cloze technique to check your reading comprehension. Complete the paragraph by filling in each blank with one of the words listed below. Each word appears in the story. Since there are five words and four blanks, one of the words will not be used.

The Hudson River is named for the navigator, Henry Hudson, who _____ it in 1609. The river rises in the Adirondack Mountains in New York State and flows 306 _____, emptying into the Atlantic Ocean. The Hudson played an important role in the early _____ of the United States. During the Revolutionary War, for example, an _____ chain was hung across the river to prevent British ships from sailing.

enormous   explored

gallantly

history   miles

	× 5 =	
NUMBER CORRECT		YOUR SCORE

	× 5 =	
NUMBER CORRECT		YOUR SCORE

LEARNING HOW TO READ CRITICALLY. The following questions check your critical thinking skills. Put an *x* in the box next to each correct answer.

1. Clues in the story suggest that the ghost rider who attacked Ichabod Crane was
   ☐ a. actually Brom Bones.
   ☐ b. the Headless Horseman of Sleepy Hollow.
   ☐ c. Hans Van Ripper.

2. After the party, Ichabod rushed out "keenly disappointed," went straight to the stable, and departed. We may infer that Ichabod was upset because
   ☐ a. he didn't like the food that had been served.
   ☐ b. he had been insulted by Brom Bones.
   ☐ c. Katrina had revealed that she wasn't interested in him.

3. It is likely that Katrina spent time with Ichabod because she
   ☐ a. was impressed with his intelligence and good looks.
   ☐ b. enjoyed his fascinating stories.
   ☐ c. wanted to make Brom Bones jealous.

4. Which statement is true?
   ☐ a. Ichabod often returned to Sleepy Hollow on late summer nights.
   ☐ b. Ichabod was hit in the head by a pumpkin.
   ☐ c. Although Ichabod pretended to be afraid of ghosts, they really didn't frighten him.

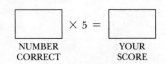

	× 5 =	
NUMBER CORRECT		YOUR SCORE

Improving Writing and Discussion Skills

• According to the author, "the name *Crane* was appropriate" to the schoolmaster. Explain in detail why this is true. The word *brunt* may be defined as "the force or shock of an attack." Why do you think the author called his character Brom Van Brunt?

• Do you believe that Ichabod deserved what happened to him? Give reasons to support your opinion.

• It is obvious why "The Legend of Sleepy Hollow" appears in a book about encounters. Select one encounter that occurs in the story. Describe it briefly but vividly.

Use the boxes below to total your scores for the exercises. Then write your score on pages 135 and 136.

	SELECTING DETAILS FROM THE STOR
+	
	KNOWING NEW VOCABULARY WORDS
+	
	IDENTIFYING STORY ELEMENTS
+	
	LOOKING AT CLOZE
+	
	LEARNING HOW TO READ CRITICALL
▼	
	Score Total: Story 1

2. The Wise and the Weak

by Philip Aponte

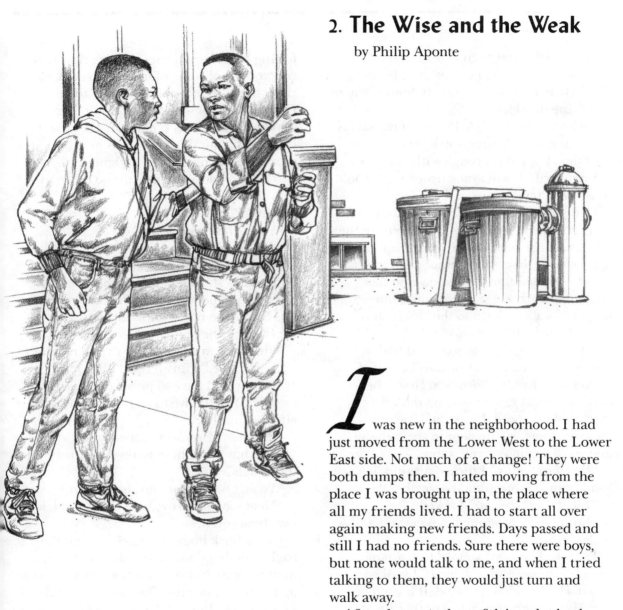

Meet the Author

Philip Aponte wrote "The Wise and the Weak" while he was still a teenager in high school. At the suggestion of his teacher, Aponte submitted the story to a national magazine. It won an award and was published. Since then it has appeared in many anthologies.

I was new in the neighborhood. I had just moved from the Lower West to the Lower East side. Not much of a change! They were both dumps then. I hated moving from the place I was brought up in, the place where all my friends lived. I had to start all over again making new friends. Days passed and still I had no friends. Sure there were boys, but none would talk to me, and when I tried talking to them, they would just turn and walk away.

After about ten days of doing absolutely nothing, I decided to do something before I went crazy. One evening after supper I went downstairs and ran across a guy sitting on the stoop. I walked up to him and said, "Hello."

"Hiya," was his reply. He started walking away. I grabbed him by his arm and asked, "Why are you walking away?"

He looked at me, then at my hand on his arm. With a wise grin on his face, he said, "You'd better get your hand off, Sonny. You're wrinkling the skin."

I released my grip. He looked at me sarcastically and said, "Better watch that, Son, or next time I might get rough with you."

I returned his sarcasm, answering, "Would you care to try?"

Flying fists, scratching fingernails, feet dancing on a human floor. I was getting the better of it. He went down. He got up. Down, up, down, up, like the continuous beat of a drum. I pushed him on his way and he staggered down the street. A smile ran across my lips. I walked down to the candy store to celebrate by buying a soda.

It was getting dark. Since I had had enough excitement for one day, I decided to go home. I walked slowly at first. Then, realizing it was rapidly getting dark, I increased my speed. I wasn't taking any chances. I opened the door to the hallway and started climbing the stairs.

"Hey you, Sonny." I turned around. It was him again, the big would-be tough guy.

"What do you want?" I asked.

"Nothing. I just wanted to meet you and make friends."

Friends. The word seemed to scare me. Yet I had to have some friends. I walked down. He extended his hand. It missed my hand but not my stomach. Another hand, not to mine but to my face. This time I went down. I got up determined to teach this "big wheel" a lesson. But now, instead of one, there were six. This time I was the one who was going up and down, and I didn't like it. It wasn't long before it was over—for me, anyway. My lips were swollen, my eye was shut, my nose was bleeding. I hesitated,

feeling for other injuries, fearing they had relieved me of some of my valuables. A hand came down to help me up. I was still away from it all. I got up and was about to say thanks. Yeah, it was him again, the "big tough guy." But this time I was in no mood— or rather, no condition—to fight.

"Come on, let's you and me go down to Vito's," he said.

"Vito's?"

"Yeah, the candy store."

"Oh, yeah, sure. Let's go."

We walked down and sat in one of the booths and started talking. I told him my life history and he told me his. His name was Ron. Nice name for a not-so-nice guy. He came to the point.

"Phil, how would you like to join our club?"

"Yeah, sure," I answered, "Why, not?"

"First, you'll have to prove you're an able member. You'll have to prove that you're efficient, useful."

"Efficient? Useful? I landed you, didn't I?"

"Yes, but you'll have to do much more than that. Well?"

"Yeah. Okay, what's my assignment?"

"Meet me tomorrow, here at Vito's, at, let's say about seven."

I went back home, entered through the back door, fixed my battered profile, and went to sleep. Nobody was home when I woke up the next morning. The day went slowly. I hadn't seen Ron all day. I hoped he wasn't joking. At six I went up and got my supper. At seven I was at Vito's. Ron hadn't arrived yet. I kept wondering what I was to do. I waited for Ron. Five after seven. Then ten after, fifteen, twenty after. He'll never come, I thought.

I was ready to leave when the door to Vito's opened. Ron came walking in, looked around, saw me. He walked over and sat down opposite me. He was mysterious, and I was jumpy. Maybe I've made a mistake, letting him think I'm bad and bold, I thought. I've never gotten in trouble before, and I wouldn't want to. I'd better go home before something really happens.

I stood up, and then Ron spoke, "Well, Phil, ready? Ready to prove yourself?"

"Well, I, I—"

"Don't worry, Phil. It has nothing to do with defying the law." I was about to say "No," when I spotted Ron's friends outside.

"Okay, Ron, let's be on our way," I said.

"Good boy, Phil." He laughed. I shook with fright. I had gone beyond my own reach. We walked until we got to the building across the street from where I lived. "Let's go up, Phil," he said.

"Yeah, sure," I answered. That was all I could say, "Yeah, sure." Up the stairs, first, second, third, and then the final floor. I stopped.

"Where are we going, Ron?"

"To the roof. You're not afraid, are you, Phil?" I didn't answer but just kept climbing. We walked out to the roof.

"Well, what now, Ron?"

"Wait a minute, just a minute." The building next to this was about five feet away. In between the two buildings was a four-floor drop. I walked to the ledge, looked over, and quickly jumped back. This I didn't like. The ledge was two feet high. Ron saw that I was jittery.

"No, let's just get on with the . . . the game."

Ron smiled. "Yeah, game." The door on the roof opened. Ron's friends emerged carrying a thick iron pipe a little over five feet long. They placed it from roof to roof. I turned to Ron.

"What's that for?"

"We're going to play Tarzan." Just then more of Ron's friends appeared on our roof.

"Tarzan. What do you mean?"

"Just what I said. You know how Tarzan swings on a rope. Well, this time it isn't going to be a rope but a bar."

"Who's going to be Tarzan?"

"I'll give you one guess."

"You're crazy, Ron. That's a four-floor drop."

"Nervous, Phil? Did I say it was going to be you?"

"No, I guess you didn't, but I have to admit you had me scared there for a minute."

"You should be, Phil, because it *is* going to be you."

I stood there, stunned, even though I had suspected it from the very beginning. If only someone would call me or come upstairs to the roof, I thought to myself. It suddenly became silent. It was the first time I had really noticed how quiet it was.

All of Ron's friends bowed politely, saying, "After you, Phil, after you." I took a few steps toward the iron bar, then stopped and turned, looking for a possible opening in their defense. The door to the roof was still open. My last chance, I thought. But Ron's thinking was faster than mine.

"You'll never make it, Phil. If you try and we catch you, we might—ah—accidently on purpose throw you over." He smiled and bowed politely, saying, "After you, Phil." I walked over to the ledge.

"Look, Ron—"

"Get going, Phil." I grabbed the end of the bar. The other end was being held by a couple of other guys. One foot went over the side—I looked down—my hand grabbed on for dear life, and this time the expression really meant something. My other foot went over. I started on my way toward the other roof, hand over hand in agony, my feet dangling in the air. My muscles ached. My hands started sweating. A little more to go. I made it. Now to put my foot on the ledge. My foot reached the ledge. Then, suddenly, without warning, one of the boys pushed it off. "Sorry," he said, "but you're not welcome on this side."

I tried again to put my foot on the ledge, but again he pushed it off. My strength, or what was left of it, was going. I pleaded with Ron to let me get over. The answer I received was a loud burst of laughter. I started back to where I had originally started. Halfway there, I felt myself slipping. I gripped tighter to the bar; I couldn't go on. Looking down, I could see nothing but darkness. I tried desperately to sit on the bar. Up I would go, then down I would slip.

I couldn't feel my hands any more. My neck muscles hurt me terribly. I tried once more, this time putting my foot on the bar, then swinging up on it. Slowly but surely I started my agonizing journey to the top. My foot was on the bar, my teeth grinding together. Up, up, up a little more. A long sigh of relief. I was sitting on the bar, drenched with sweat. It was silent again. A few sounds, minutes. A plane passed overhead, but I didn't dare look up. Why? I didn't know, nor did I care to think about it.

"Look, Ron, what now, please? Please let me go." A few tears slid down my face. I wasn't one of them. I guess I had known it from the beginning.

"Well, Ron, well?"

"Hey, Phil, you want a glass of water or something? You want to play cards? Come on." He laughed. They all laughed. But when you're in death's grasp, you don't laugh. "Well, Phil, we're going."

"Wait, Ron. If you go, I'll never get out of here."

"Look, Phil, if you get out of this, you're one of the boys. If you don't,—well . . ." He smiled and left, his boys following.

If I swung to one end, the other end would become unbalanced and would be likely to slide off. Another puzzle to figure out. I thought of one solution, then another, and another. No good, no good. None of them were any good. I thought of every possible angle. The only thing to do was to hope the bar wouldn't slide off the roof.

Again I hung from the center of the bar and inched up toward the ledge.

The bar started slipping. I reached for the ledge, grabbed it as the bar fell clanging below. The little pebbles of the ledge were cutting into my fingertips, but I was close. My arms extended high over my head. My body was close against the building. I lifted myself, scraping my knees and my face. Home was so near, so near. My foot reached for the ledge. One last burst of energy, and over I went, flat on my back on the roof. I lay there, my eyes closed, my legs and arms dead to the world.

I stayed there for what seemed hours. Then slowly I went back home, making sure I wasn't seen. Not much later we moved to another place. Not much of a change. Both dumps, but it was a change for me—plenty.

SELECTING DETAILS FROM THE STORY.
The following questions help you check your reading comprehension. Put an *x* in the box next to each correct answer.

1. When he moved to the Lower East side, Phil was eager to
   - ☐ a. get a job.
   - ☐ b. explore the new neighborhood.
   - ☐ c. find some new friends.

2. The gang forced Phil to go to
   - ☐ a. a candy store.
   - ☐ b. the roof of a building.
   - ☐ c. his house.

3. While Phil was struggling on the bar, the boys
   - ☐ a. teased him.
   - ☐ b. tried to help him.
   - ☐ c. let him join their club.

4. At the end of the story, Phil
   - ☐ a. complained to the police.
   - ☐ b. fought with the gang.
   - ☐ c. moved to a different place.

KNOWING NEW VOCABULARY WORDS. The following questions check your vocabulary skills. Put an *x* in the box next to each correct answer.

1. Phil walked to the ledge on the roof, saw there was a four-floor drop, and jumped back, feeling jittery. What is the meaning of the word *jittery*?
   - ☐ a. confident
   - ☐ b. nervous
   - ☐ c. contented

2. After the fight, Phil went home and fixed his battered profile. As used here, the word *profile* means
   - ☐ a. face.
   - ☐ b. reputation.
   - ☐ c. boxing gloves.

3. Ron told Phil not to worry—that proving himself had nothing to do with defying the law. The word *defying* means
   - ☐ a. opposing or challenging.
   - ☐ b. obeying or following.
   - ☐ c. learning or studying.

4. He hung onto the rod, dangling in agony between the buildings. Which phrase best defines the word *agony*?
   - ☐ a. much hope
   - ☐ b. great enjoyment
   - ☐ c. painful suffering

☐ × 5 = ☐

NUMBER CORRECT   YOUR SCORE

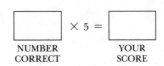

☐ × 5 = ☐

NUMBER CORRECT   YOUR SCORE

23

IDENTIFYING STORY ELEMENTS. The following questions check your knowledge of story elements. Put an *x* in the box next to each correct answer.

1. Who is the *main character* in "The Wise and the Weak"?
   - ☐ a. Ron
   - ☐ b. Phil
   - ☐ c. Vito

2. What happened first in the *plot* of the story?
   - ☐ a. Phil reached for the ledge and pulled himself up.
   - ☐ b. Ron asked Phil if he wanted to join the club.
   - ☐ c. Phil and Ron got into a fight.

3. The *mood* of "The Wise and the Weak" is
   - ☐ a. serious.
   - ☐ b. comical.
   - ☐ c. mysterious.

4. Which statement best expresses the *theme* of the story?
   - ☐ a. When he moves to a new neighborhood, a young man has a dangerous and terrifying experience.
   - ☐ b. It can be difficult to make friends with people you don't know very well.
   - ☐ c. A young man tries to prove that he is mean and tough.

LOOKING AT CLOZE. The following questions use the cloze technique to check your reading comprehension. Complete the paragraph by filling in each blank with one of the words listed below. Each word appears in the story. Since there are five words and four blanks, one of the words will not be used.

Have you ever used the _____,
1

"With friends like you, who needs enemies"?

If so, you probably _____ that
2

someone you counted on for help was not

willing to assist you. A discovery like this

can be _____ disappointing.
3

Because when you're looking for aid, it's true

that "A friend in need is a _____
4

indeed."

realized   terribly

expression

drenched   friend

☐ × 5 = ☐

NUMBER   YOUR
CORRECT   SCORE

☐ × 5 = ☐

NUMBER   YOUR
CORRECT   SCORE

LEARNING HOW TO READ CRITICALLY.
The following questions check your critical
thinking skills. Put an *x* in the box next to
each correct answer.

1. We may infer that Ron arranged "the
   game" because he
   - ☐ a. hoped that Phil would become a
     member of the gang.
   - ☐ b. wanted to get even with Phil for
     beating him in a fight.
   - ☐ c. thought that Phil would enjoy the
     challenge.

2. Which statement is true?
   - ☐ a. Phil cheerfully accompanied the
     gang to the roof.
   - ☐ b. If Phil had tried to run, he would
     probably have succeeded in getting
     away.
   - ☐ c. The gang almost killed Phil.

3. At the end of the story Phil went back
   home "making sure I wasn't seen." Probably,
   Phil returned secretly because he
   - ☐ a. was very modest.
   - ☐ b. wanted to avoid meeting the gang.
   - ☐ c. didn't want his family to know where
     he had been.

4. The final sentence of the story suggests
   that Phil
   - ☐ a. was glad to leave the neighborhood.
   - ☐ b. was sorry to leave the neighborhood.
   - ☐ c. had several other encounters with
     the gang.

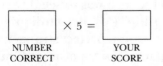

NUMBER
CORRECT

× 5 =

YOUR
SCORE

Improving Writing and Discussion Skills

- Why do you think the story is called
  "The Wise and the Weak"? Think
  of another interesting and appropriate name for the selection. Use
  the word "Encounter" in your title.
- Suppose that Phil had told Ron he
  didn't want to join the club. How
  do you think the story might have
  ended?
- Ron forced Phil to play a game that
  was both deadly and cruel. Why do
  you think the other boys agreed to
  go along with Ron's "game"? Do you
  think that Phil will eventually forget
  about the experience on the roof—
  or is he likely to remember it vividly
  forever? Explain your answer.

Use the boxes below to total your scores
for the exercises. Then write your score on
pages 135 and 136.

SELECTING DETAILS FROM THE STORY

+

KNOWING NEW VOCABULARY WORDS

+

IDENTIFYING STORY ELEMENTS

+

LOOKING AT CLOZE

+

LEARNING HOW TO READ CRITICALLY

▼

Score Total: Story 2

3. **Dear Marsha**

by Judie Angell

July 13

*D*ear Anne Marie,

I guess this letter is probably a big surprise to you . . . I mean, you probably looked at the return address and sign-off and all and saw that it's from nobody you ever heard of, right? Well, here's the reason I'm writing.

Maybe you remember this assignment that the kids in our English class got back in February. Our teacher (Ms. Bernardi, maybe that rings a bell) wrote to your English teacher and she asked him if he'd like to do this experiment: He would send a list of all the kids in your class with their names and addresses and we would pick those names out of a hat and write a letter to the name we picked. See, you all lived far away and the idea was to see if we could form a "relationship" (Ms. Bernardi grew up in the sixties) with a perfect stranger, using only pen and paper. (Or typewriter, I mean, *you*

Meet the Author

Judie Angell (1937–) is one of today's most popular writers of books for children and young adults. Her humorous and touching novels and short stories have been enjoyed by countless numbers of readers. Among Angell's books are *The Buffalo Nickel Blues Band, A Word from Our Sponsor,* and *Suds.* Angell was born in New York City and is a former elementary schoolteacher. She currently lives with her family in South Salem, New York.

know.) Anyway, Ms. Bernardi said she wasn't going to grade the assignment, or even see it or anything because this assignment was personal, just for ourselves. You know, to "express ourselves" with a perfect stranger. Whatever. So naturally, if it didn't mean a grade or anything, I didn't do it.

But the thing is—I picked your name out of the hat and I just sort of kept it, you know, and now it's summer and hot and practically all of my friends are away, so . . . Here's a letter. You're a stranger even if you may not be perfect (or maybe you are perfect, I don't know), but here I am, trying to form this "relationship" using only two fingers on the typewriter (please excuse the mistakes, I'm taking Business Typing next semester) and you're the one I'm supposed to try it with.

Well, I'm not going to say anything more until I hear back from you—Hope you turn out to be cool.

Your new pen pal (maybe)
Marsha

July 18
Dear Marsha,
Your letter was great! It really picked up a slow summer for me.

I remember that assignment. Some of the kids really got into it when they got letters from your class and they're still writing back and forth. The friendships are terrific because everybody feels safe with them, you know? I mean, because we're so far away no one knows anyone the pen pal knows. And since you never have to meet, you feel freer to say whatever you want with no one coming down on you or whatever, you know.

So I'm glad you wrote and I'm also glad

it's now instead of then, because back in Feb. I was really *wiped,* I mean really. See, my dad died, it wasn't sudden or anything, he was sick a long time, but still it was very hard on everybody as you can probably figure out. So now it's just my mom and my sister and me and . . . we miss Dad, so sometimes we get on each other's nerves.

I guess if you wanted me to be the first one to give out personal stuff I guess there's that. Plus . . . let's see . . . If you're thinking about "m-e-n," I don't go out a whole lot, but there's one guy I like at school. The thing is, he's *younger* than I am and I get embarrassed about that and since he doesn't even know I like him . . . I guess you can't count it as a "relationship." (That word bugs me too.)

I hope this is enough for you to think that maybe we could be friends, and I like the idea of a pen pal.

From
Anne Marie

July 21
Dear Anne Marie,
You are *definitely* the coolest person! I couldn't wait to hear back from you so I'm writing you the same day I got your letter.

I'm sorry about your dad. That must be tough to deal with. I mean, I have both of my parents and it never occurred to me that one of them could die. I know that sounds stupid, but I just never thought about it. They're okay most of the time, but really, I guess I just take them for granted, to be honest about it.

So now I'll tell you more about myself.

I'm a senior in high school, or at least I will be starting September. Which is okay, because the sooner I graduate the sooner

I can start My Life. My dad says I could go to college if I want (*he's* the one who really wants me to go), but I'm not sure I could stand all that much school. I'm thinking about it more this summer, though, because I have this job at our local five-and-ten as a checkout girl and if anything is bor-ing, that is *it*! Here's what you get: "Marsha, last week you had green grosgrain[1] in the sewing department and now it isn't there, why *not*?" And—"Mar-sha, you took ten minutes extra for lunch yesterday and it came off *my* time, so you better come back ten minutes early today." That kind of stuff. Borrrrr-ing.

Okay, well—I'm five feet five inches tall, which is about average, I guess, and I have black hair which in this weather I wear either in a chignon (sp.?) or in a ponytail. It's pretty long and straight and I guess it's my nicest feature. I'm a cheerleader and I think my hair looks good flopping up and down when I jump. (I'm not really as conceited as that sounds!) Also I have brown eyes and no-more-BRACES. I'm pretty thin, which isn't too great when you wear a bathing suit. What do you look like? I picture Anne Marie as a blonde.

I don't have a boyfriend right now, although there's a very nice guy who works in the stockroom at the five-and-ten. Hmmm . . . maybe. . . .

Most of my friends got jobs at resorts and hotels in the mountains. I should have applied to one of them but as usual I was late and lazy, so here I am, bored at the five-and-ten. Write soon.

Your friend,
Marsha

---

1. **grosgrain:** a kind of cloth, often used for ribbons.

July 25

Dear Marsha,

Boy, do I know what you mean about boredom! I'm working part time at my school—office stuff, and the rest of the time I'm at home because my mom and sister really need for us all to be together. Your town sounds like the same kind of hick burg mine is. You have one movie house and it's just got around to showing talkies, right? And: one Laundromat, a drugstore (NO BARE FEET, THIS MEANS YOU), a post office, and if you're real lucky, one of those no-alcohol bars for kids to hang out in on weekends.

One nice thing here, though—there is a lake we can go to. In fact, our family has always had a cabin there. It's called Lake Michigan, which was someone's idea of a joke, because it's more of a pond than a lake and it has a lot more brambly woods than pond. But this summer no one in my house seems to have the energy for going up there a lot.

I'm a little shorter than you—five two exactly—and I do have blondish-brownish hair that's short and curly. I always wanted long black hair like yours. You sound really pretty and I bet that guy in the stockroom notices you pretty soon! I used to wear glasses but I got contacts finally and I think I look better now. Wish I had more to write but I don't, so let's hope things start to get more exciting for both of us!

Love,
Anne Marie

August 2

Dear Anne Marie,

It took me a while before I could write again. It's not that I didn't want to, but some stuff happened and I've been kind of scared and depressed ever since.

What happened was, this girl at work—she's the one I was kidding about in my last letter, the one who complains about my coming back late from lunch. Her name is Claudia and we alternate shifts. Anyway, when I realized she was actually counting every one of my lunchtime minutes, I started coming back really on time, you know? Sometimes, even early. Well, last week when I relieved her, I counted up the receipts and the money in the register and stuff and it seemed to me that I was coming up short. The receipts and the money didn't check out, you know? But I figured it was me, I must've done something wrong. I mean, my math is hardly the greatest. So I let it go and when Claudia came back at four o'clock, I told her to check it out. So she did and said I was wrong and dumb and everything was okay and blah, blah, blah. But the next thing I know, Mrs. Handy, the manager, started checking everything between shifts because she said we were losing some money.

Listen, I won't drag this on, but accusations were thrown around and Claudia accused me of stealing. That was when I caught on that she was the one who was stealing and I knew that one time I got back too early for her to be able to hide it.

Well, of course she said I was the one and since it was her word against mine and she's a full-time worker and I'm only part time and no one noticed any shortage before I got there—naturally I got blamed. I wasn't arrested or anything because no one could prove I did it, but I did get fired. And as you put it so well, this *is* a hick burg, and I stand about as much chance of getting another job as I have of spreading wings and flying away. Which I'd sure like to do. I really didn't steal, Anne Marie. I hope you believe me. The cute boy in the stockroom sure doesn't. You should have seen the look he gave me.

So . . . things got exciting for a while, anyway.

Love,
Marsha

August 5

Dear Marsha,

I got your letter and broke into tears, I swear I did. Of course I believe you didn't steal anything. But they will find out eventually. Claudia won't stop stealing and I bet she does the same thing with the next person they hire and they will all catch on.

I feel so bad for you, I don't know what to say. After I read your letter I told my mom and sister that I just had to get away for a while, so I took the bus up to our cabin and that's where I am now. I'm sitting on the porch and looking out at (ha-ha) Lake Michigan and thinking about you. People can be so mean. But I bet there are lots of people in the town who know you well enough to know it was all a lie and will be glad to hire you.

It's so peaceful up here, really. Just about an hour and fifteen minutes north of my house, but it feels like another world. Wait a minute, Marsha. . . .

You won't believe it! I'm back now, but I had to go inside and close the windows and doors and spray everything with Lysol! While I was sitting there describing all the peace and quiet, this SKUNK marches right up on the porch and lets me have some of what skunks do best! YUUUUCH! This is just AWFUL, did you ever get a whiff of skunk?

They say tomato juice takes the smell away, but I don't have any and what are you supposed to do, bathe in it or what? PEEEEW!

So I'm sitting here in this locked cabin wondering which smells worse, the Lysol or the skunk or the mixture of both, and thinking of you.

Love,
Anne Marie

August 10

Dear Anne Marie,

Your letter gave me the first good laugh I've had in a while! I'm still laughing because I think I can smell that combination of stuff you mentioned on the pages of the letter! You can't even imagine how much I wish I had a place to go like Lake Michigan (without the skunk!) but we're pretty far from any quiet place with water and woods. I mean, there's a pool at the town recreation center, but that's not exactly what I had in mind. The closest I can get to coolness and peace and quiet is my basement, but *that* smells of cat litter and Clorox, *almost* as bad as your place!

Well, my mom and dad believe I didn't take any money or anything else, but it's hard for them because everyone they know heard about what happened. And so when people say, "Oh, Marsha, wasn't that awful, we just *know* you'd never" and all that, I somehow get the feeling they're really thinking Maybe she did, you know these kids today. . . .

Anyway, tell me something good to cheer me up. Your letters are the only nice thing to happen this whole stinking summer!—NO PUN INTENDED!

Love,
Marsha

August 16

Dear Marsha,

I hope by the time this gets to you that you're feeling better. I want you to know I really do think about you all the time.

Maybe this will cheer you up a little. . . . Did you ever have a carnival come to your town? Our firehouse sits on a tract of land of about twelve acres and every year they put on a really terrific carnival. Picture this: There's a high booth on wheels with a glass window where you can watch a boy spin pink cotton candy around and around. Close your eyes now, and you can smell it, all sickly sweet and gorgeous, and you can make mustaches and beards and eyebrows and earrings all over your face with it, you know? And they also have this huge plastic bubble, all different colors, with a foam bottom and you can go in there and jump your heart out. You fall over a lot, of course, but you don't get hurt even if you fall on your face because it's so soft. And there are these booths where you can throw baseballs at little Indian tepees and win neat stuff like plush polar bear dolls and clock radios and blow-dryers with three speeds and makeup mirrors and everything. And best of all is the Ferris wheel, because they stop it for a few minutes when you get to the top, and it's like you really are on top of the world. So picture yourself on top of the world and that's where you'll be.

That's where I was last night. And when I got to the top I thought about you and made a wish, so I know things will get better soon for you.

And also, guess what? At the shooting gallery, guess who I met? The younger guy I told you about. And we went on the Whip together. And I'm going back tonight, so . . . who knows?

Love,
Anne Marie

August 20

Dear Anne Marie,

I have read your letter about eight hundred times. Where you live sounds so great. I pictured the carnival. I really tasted the cotton candy. I won a stuffed bear. I rode on the Ferris wheel with you and I think the "younger man" is cute. I liked being on top of the world, even if it was only for a few minutes.

Things here only seem to be getting worse. One of my girlfriends is back from her hotel job and you wouldn't believe how she sounded on the phone when I called her up. I feel like everyone's looking at me whenever I walk down the street.

Now I'm seriously starting to think about college, if only to get away from here. My dad says he's sorry it took something like this to get me thinking about it, but he's glad I am, he says. A blessing in disguise, he says. Ha, some blessing! But even if I do go to college, I still have a year of high school left and I honestly don't know how I'm going to stand it.

Tell me something else to smell and taste and ride on.

Love,
Marsha

August 25

Dear Marsha,

I think it's neat you're thinking about college. If you're lucky enough to be able to go, I really think that's what you should do. It's just my opinion, but that's what I think.

Marsha, did you ever see kittens being born? You have *never* seen anything so incredible in your whole life! My Y-M (younger man) works at his dad's carpentry shop in the summer and they have this mama cat who was about to give birth and he asked me if I'd like to watch. Well, it took from six o'clock to around ten. The mama had a litter of seven kittens, and they came out two, two, one and two, over all those four hours. They each came out wrapped in a shiny silver cover, which the mama licked up and ate. I know it sounds really gross, but it was honestly beautiful. Their teeny eyes were shut tight and they made these little squeaky noises and they looked at first as if they had no fur, but they do. Y-M says I can have one.

Keep thinking about college and you'll see how quickly the year will go.

Love,
Anne Marie

September 1

Dear Anne Marie,

It's Labor Day weekend and I'm spending it crying. The cheerleading squad is meeting Tuesday, the day before school starts and I'm "not welcome" on it anymore. I got the word straight from the captain herself. "Oh, I don't believe any of it, Marsha" she says, "but you know how people think of cheerleaders, they're supposed to represent the school's highest standards" and blah, blah, blah! "I know you'll sacrifice," she says, "for the good of the school." Right. Can you *believe* it? Anne Marie, it's *so* not fair!

Well, I can't handle it, Anne Marie, I really

can't. I just can't spend an entire year at school like this. So I've made this decision, and I just know being the kind of person you are and with the kind of family you say you have, that you might be happy about it. This decision, I mean.

I know my mom and dad are on my side, but they're not, you know, the same as a *friend* or anything. And this summer, I guess you know that you became my very best friend.

I want to be where I can sit on top of the world on a Ferris wheel and watch little kittens being born and chase skunks away from a cabin porch. And spend all my time with a true friend, who's sensitive and caring and growing up with the same kind of feelings I have. That stupid school assignment was the best thing that ever happened to me, Anne Marie, and I know I'm dragging this out, but here's my idea:

Could I spend the year with you? I swear on my own life I won't be any trouble, in fact, I'll be a help. With your dad gone, I can help make up for the work he did around the house. I'm very handy, I really am, I can do all kinds of things.

And best of all, we could go to school together, and do our homework together, and sit up nights and talk, and bake stuff and double date and go to the prom and make Senior Year everything it's supposed to be! And I'll bring my tapes—I bet I have the best rock and roll tape collection you ever heard!

Don't you think it would be great? Don't you? School's starting next week, Anne Marie. . . . Please let me know. . . .

Love,
Marsha

WESTERN UNION NIGHT LETTER
TUES SEPT 5

DEAR MARSHA—YOU MUST STAY IN SCHOOL, RIGHT THERE IN YOUR OWN TOWN—IT WILL BE HARD, VERY HARD, BUT YOU MUST DO IT—REMEMBER, YOU DIDN'T DO ANYTHING WRONG AND THEREFORE YOU MUST NOT RUN AWAY—YOU MUST NEVER LET STUPID AND CRUEL PEOPLE GET THE BEST OF YOU—I AM SURE YOUR MOM AND DAD HAVE TOLD YOU THE SAME—HOLD YOUR HEAD UP AS HIGH AS YOU CAN AND GIVE THAT CHEER-LEADING SQUAD A GOOD RASPBERRY—

MARSHA, I CANNOT TELL YOU HOW SORRY I AM FOR THIS—MY NAME WAS NOT SUPPOSED TO BE INCLUDED IN THAT LIST YOUR TEACHER RECEIVED FROM OUR TEACHER—SOMEONE MUST HAVE PUT IT IN AS A JOKE—BUT I DIDN'T MIND BECAUSE YOUR FIRST LETTERS WERE SUCH A JOY THAT I SIMPLY HAD TO ANSWER THEM IN KIND—THEN WHEN YOUR TROUBLE BEGAN, ALL I WANTED WAS TO MAKE YOU FEEL BETTER—MARSHA, I HOPE YOU WON'T MIND THIS—I HOPE IT DOESN'T MAKE ANY DIFFERENCE TO YOU—I HOPE WE CAN CONTINUE TO WRITE AND BE FRIENDS—

DEAR MARSHA, MY DAD DID DIE LAST WINTER AND I DO LIVE WITH MY MOTHER AND SISTER—THEY ARE EIGHTY-THREE AND SIXTY-THREE, RESPECTIVELY—I'M THE PRINCIPAL OF OUR SCHOOL AND I'M SIXTY-ONE YEARS OLD—

ALL MY BEST LOVE,
ANNE MARIE

SELECTING DETAILS FROM THE STORY.
The following questions help you check your reading comprehension. Put an *x* in the box next to each correct answer.

1. Marsha began to write to Anne Marie as a result of
   - ☐ a. having met her the previous summer.
   - ☐ b. having gotten her name from a friend.
   - ☐ c. an assignment suggested by Marsha's English teacher.

2. In her first letter, Anne Marie told Marsha that
   - ☐ a. her father died recently.
   - ☐ b. she was popular and dated a lot.
   - ☐ c. she didn't care much for the idea of having a pen pal.

3. The captain of the cheerleading squad said that Marsha
   - ☐ a. should join the squad the day before school starts.
   - ☐ b. was not welcome on the squad anymore.
   - ☐ c. could be a member of the squad if somebody dropped out.

4. In her last letter to Anne Marie, Marsha asked if
   - ☐ a. she could spend the year with Anne Marie.
   - ☐ b. Anne Marie could visit her soon.
   - ☐ c. Anne Marie thought that she stole the money.

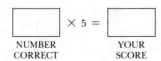

NUMBER CORRECT   × 5 =   YOUR SCORE

KNOWING NEW VOCABULARY WORDS.
The following questions check your vocabulary skills. Put an *x* in the box next to each correct answer.

1. Although she said she was a cheerleader with long black hair, Marsha took care not to sound conceited. The word *conceited* means
   - ☐ a. vain.
   - ☐ b. athletic.
   - ☐ c. friendly.

2. It took Marsha awhile before she could write because something upsetting occurred and she felt "kind of scared and depressed." The word *depressed* means
   - ☐ a. pleased or delighted.
   - ☐ b. sad and gloomy.
   - ☐ c. wild and reckless.

3. After it was discovered that money was missing, "accusations were tossed around," and Marsha was blamed and then fired. Which of the following best defines the word *accusations*?
   - ☐ a. words of support
   - ☐ b. messages of concern
   - ☐ c. charges that someone has broken the law

4. The firehouse was situated on a tract of land about twelve acres large. Define the word *tract* as used in this sentence.
   - ☐ a. structure
   - ☐ b. grass
   - ☐ c. area

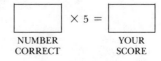

NUMBER CORRECT   × 5 =   YOUR SCORE

IDENTIFYING STORY ELEMENTS. The following questions check your knowledge of story elements. Put an *x* in the box next to each correct answer.

1. What happened last in the *plot* of the story?
   - ☐ a. Claudia accused Marsha of stealing some money.
   - ☐ b. Marsha explained that she picked Anne Marie's name out of a hat.
   - ☐ c. Anne Marie stated that she was sixty-one years old.

2. Which of the following statements best illustrates *character development*?
   - ☐ a. At the beginning of the story Anne Marie was a stranger to Marsha; at the end of the story Marsha considered Anne Marie her best friend.
   - ☐ b. At first Marsha thought that she wouldn't write to a pen pal; later she decided to write to Anne Marie.
   - ☐ c. First Marsha was fired from her job; later people didn't seem to trust her.

3. What is striking about the *style* of "Dear Marsha"?
   - ☐ a. The characters never express their feelings.
   - ☐ b. The story is told entirely through letters.
   - ☐ c. The story contains no slang expressions.

4. Which phrase best *characterizes* Anne Marie?
   - ☐ a. thoughtless and unconcerned
   - ☐ b. sensitive and caring
   - ☐ c. disagreeable and unkind

	× 5 =	
NUMBER CORRECT		YOUR SCORE

LOOKING AT CLOZE. The following questions use the cloze technique to check your reading comprehension. Complete the paragraph by filling in each blank with one of the words listed below. Each word appears in the story. Since there are five words and four blanks, one of the words will not be used.

Labor Day, as the name suggests, is a holiday that honors _____ people. Observed on the first Monday in _____ , it signals, for many, the end of summer. The _____ Labor Day parade was held in New York City in 1882. Twelve years later President Grover Cleveland signed a bill making Labor Day a national holiday and creating a three-day _____ .

weekend   assignment

working

September   first

	× 5 =	
NUMBER CORRECT		YOUR SCORE

LEARNING HOW TO READ CRITICALLY.
The following questions check your critical
thinking skills. Put an *x* in the box next to
each correct answer.

1. Which statement is true?
   - ☐ a. Marsha didn't care about what
     people thought of her.
   - ☐ b. Marsha was actually guilty of
     stealing the money.
   - ☐ c. Marsha might be considered a victim
     of small-town gossip.

2. Anne Marie probably felt obliged to reveal
   that she was a principal when
   - ☐ a. Marsha pleaded to spend some time
     with her.
   - ☐ b. some of Marsha's friends hinted that
     that was the case.
   - ☐ c. Marsha began to suspect that the
     letters were written by an adult.

3. We may infer that Marsha considered
   Anne Marie her best friend because
   - ☐ a. Marsha felt very comfortable sharing
     her feelings and thoughts with her.
   - ☐ b. Marsha and Anne Marie enjoyed
     so many good times together.
   - ☐ c. Anne Marie said that Marsha was
     her best friend.

4. Anne Marie probably sent her last message
   by Western Union because she
   - ☐ a. was too embarrassed to send a
     regular letter.
   - ☐ b. felt her message was urgent.
   - ☐ c. had lost or forgotten Marsha's address.

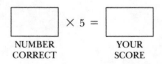

NUMBER
CORRECT
    × 5 =   YOUR
SCORE

Improving Writing and Discussion Skills

- In her last message Anne Marie said,
  "I hope we can continue to write and
  be friends." Do you think that will
  happen? Explain your response.
- Do you agree with all the advice that
  Anne Marie gave Marsha? With some
  of the advice? Explain. Anne Marie
  suggested that Marsha "give that
  cheerleading squad a good raspberry." What is the meaning of that
  expression? (If necessary, refer to the
  word *raspberry* in the dictionary.)
- Suppose that you are Marsha. Think
  carefully about Anne Marie's last message. Then write a letter in response.
  Try to make your letter sound like one
  that Marsha might write.

Use the boxes below to total your scores
for the exercises. Then write your score on
pages 135 and 136.

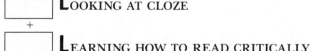

SELECTING DETAILS FROM THE STORY

+

KNOWING NEW VOCABULARY WORDS

+

IDENTIFYING STORY ELEMENTS

+

LOOKING AT CLOZE

+

LEARNING HOW TO READ CRITICALLY

▼

Score Total: Story 3

4. Polar Night

by Norah Burke

Meet the Author

Norah Burke (1907–) was born in England but spent her early years there and in India, where her father served as an officer in the army. Her autobiography, *Jungle Child*, provides much information about the social life and customs of India at that time. Burke has written several novels and many short stories. "Polar Night" is her best-known work.

As the hot arctic summer drew to a close, the polar bear knew that a hard time lay ahead for her. During the months of night, when it was always fifty degrees below zero, her cubs would be born. The great task of motherhood had already begun.

The time was coming soon when she would bury herself deep down under the snow to give birth. From that day until the day when she and the cubs pushed their way up into daylight again, she would not eat. She and they must live on what she had stored in her body during the summer—and on what she could catch and eat now. She must fatten herself up for the ordeal, and there was not much time left.

At the moment she was hunting along the edge of the ice because where there was water there were seals. There were also fish and the chance of a porpoise or walrus. As winter turned the roots and berries and seaweed of the polar islands into glass, the bears moved to the ice-edge for their food.

This was the arctic region, the area north of the limit of tree growth. It was a landscape of snow and ice, of drifting icebergs, all in constant motion. In summer the gulls and other birds filled the air with noise. But now all that the bear could hear was the splash of blue water against the grinding ice.

Under the dark sky on the white land, she was part of the lonely, desolate landscape. Powerful and dangerous, she was the largest of bears. She could swim forty miles out to sea if necessary. She ruled her kingdom— the arctic—and no natural enemy challenged her reign. Now, her feet gripped the ice, carrying her huge weight silently, while her low swinging head searched the ice for food.

She was not clearly aware of what was happening in her body, but her instinct told her to love the unborn cubs—to prepare for them and protect them. She did not risk her body in careless adventures as she would have at other times.

But food? Food—

Suddenly, far down the ice field, she saw a black dot on the ice—a seal. It was essential to catch him. In a moment she had decided on her approach. She slipped silently into the water to cut off his line of retreat. The ice rocked as her great weight left it.

The bear was as much at home in the water as on land. She swam like a dog—on top of the water or submerged—and the water was much warmer than the air on her face. Keeping under the shoulder of ice, she got near to the seal. Breathing carefully, she slid nearer and nearer, ready to spring—to dive—

Suddenly the seal saw her. Terror twisted his face. A moment of awful indecision— should he plunge into the sea, his natural line of escape, and perhaps fall straight into her jaws? Or should he struggle across the ice to that other hole—?

He swung away from her, dragging himself madly along. The bear lunged out of the water onto the ice.

The water splashed off her everywhere like a tidal wave. There was a flurry of snow and water and fighting seal. His quick, struggling body flapped as she slew him. Blood spurted onto the snow.

When the seal was dead, the bear attended to herself. She got rid of the wet from her coat before it could freeze. She shook and the drops flew off in rainbows in all directions. She rolled and nosed along in the snow. She wiped her sides, her chin, and soon all was dry.

Now for the seal. She ripped up the body, turning back the skin and blubber, letting out a cloud of steam. Greedily she ate of the hot crimson meat. Seal meat was her favorite, full of flavor and warm, not like the white, icy flakes of cod.

Then, although the bear had no natural enemies, she stopped suddenly as she ate. She lifted her head, looked, listened, and scented. Blood dripped from her chin onto the snow.

There was nothing.

All the same, she obeyed her instinct. Leaving the rest of the meal, she slipped into the water. It was warmer there and easier to move.

Soon she saw seals walking upright, coming along the shore. These upright seals, these land-seals, were rare creatures and dangerous, even though they were so weak. The places they lived in had light and noise and smelled full of good food. The she-bear often came near their places, attracted by the smells. She hunted these land-seals too and ate them when she could. They were not like the sea-seals, though. They wore seal fur, but they did not taste the same as sea-seals.

They, in turn, hunted bear, as the she-bear knew well. She had seen white, empty skins hanging up in their camps and had smelled the dark red meat cooking.

Now, as she watched the approaching men, she thought about whether or not to kill them. But the unborn life in her said get away. So she dived and swam out of their range.

In the next few days, the bear gorged on fish and seal. No longer did the summer provide good-tasting moss, and berries and roots. She dived into the cold blue ocean for her food.

But now the arctic day was over. Birds silently flew south. Then came the freezing of the sea. Crystals formed beneath the surface, and needles of ice joined together, thickening, hardening, adding more ice to the mountains of ice already there. The polar night began.

Now the real cold came. Now the food disappeared, and old male bears grew thin and savage.

The she-bear chose her den.

There was a huge range of ice that had been pushed up into mountains. Behind this curtain of ice she found a great cave, packed with snow.

This was the place.

Her body was ready now for the ordeal. Thick fat, gathered from seal and fish, lined her skin.

She burrowed down into the snow on the floor of the cave. The snow was so light that the wind blew it about like feathers, and she could breathe in it. She burrowed deeper and deeper. She curled and rolled herself round and round, pushing the snow, packing it, shaping the dean. All the sides of it melted with her heat, then froze again into slippery walls. Her hot breath passed up through the way she had dug. It melted the sides of the channel, leaving a tube that would supply her with air until she came up again in the spring.

Inside the snow and ice—inside her thick, oily fur and the layer of blubber, she was warm, fully fed, and sleepy. She slept and waited.

Time passed—and then the first familiar pang of birth trembled in her stomach. Pain fluttered like a butterfly and was gone.

She stirred, lifted her head, rearranged herself.

The pain came again, stronger, longer. She moved uneasily.

Then it was there—hard, forcing, pushing, out of her control. She grunted, tensed all her muscles, pressed and gasped. Another tremor of pain—and the first cub was born.

A wave of relief relaxed her.

There he lay whimpering, so wet and tiny, hardly alive. She nuzzled him delightedly and started to clean him up.

But now another tremor—the same long, final one as before, though easier—and the second cub was born.

It was over now. She felt calmer, and the pain diminished, faded away.

She licked and licked them, turning them over, rolling and caressing them. Life strengthened in them as they dried, as they fed.

Meanwhile in the world above, the sun had returned. Deep in the snow cave, the bear knew it as the snow glistened, grew luminous with the light shining through.

Then one day the bear heard voices. The

snow above vibrated with footsteps. The ice ceiling cracked.

She rose and stood ready in case the land-seals—the seals who walked upright—saw the warm, yellow air holes that marked her den, in case one of them fell in.

She stood fierce, ready to defend her cubs.

Gradually the voices and the footsteps faded away.

Soon it was time to come out into the world again. The cubs' eyes were open, their coats grown. They were walking, getting stronger every day. Now they must come out and face the world and swim and fight and catch seals. There was everything to teach them, and while they were still learning—still babies, they had to be kept safe and fed. All this she had to do alone. Other years she'd had a mate to help her, but this time he was gone—lost—the upright seals had attacked, had killed him.

She began to tear her way out of the cave. Her giant paws and black nails broke open the ice walls of their den. The ice gave way and snow fell in.

They climbed out.

Clean, frozen air, dazzling with sun, hit them like the stroke of an ax.

The arctic landscape blazed white and blue. Everything hit them at once—light, noise, wind—the blast of a new world.

The mother bear plunged joyfully into the water. All the dirt and staleness of winter were washed away. It was like flight. She plunged and rose and shook and plunged again in sheer joy, feeling so fresh, so clean, the cold saltwater running through her teeth.

Then she returned to the cubs. They were sitting on the edge, squeaking with fright. She began urging them to come in. They moved slowly forward, then scrambled back.

Suddenly one ventured too far down the ice and slithered, shrieking, into the sea, where he bobbed up a moment later like a cork.

His brother, seeing this, gained courage and plunged in too.

They found that they could swim.

Presently she pushed them up onto the ice again where they shook and dried. The next thing was food. She left them while she killed a seal, and the three of them ate it.

After that there were lessons—how to fish, how to kill. Living was difficult at first, for three hunters cannot move as silently as one, but they got along.

Then one day land-seals approached them, unseen, from behind an ice ridge. The first they knew of it was an explosion, and one cub gasped and doubled up as he was hit. The bears dived for the water, even the little wounded one. He managed to keep up with them. His mother and brother would die rather than desert him.

They all swam on, but slowly—slowly. Both cubs were still so small and slow, and they must hurry—

Blood ran in the water.

Other shots spattered around them.

Anxiety roared in the she-bear's blood. Her heart was pounding. She pushed the cubs on, and turned to meet her enemies. She reared up onto the ice and galloped toward them, a charge that nothing could stop—not even death—if they'd stayed to face it, but they turned and ran.

The bear returned to her cubs.

The wounded one was sinking lower and lower in the water, but she managed to push him onto the ice at last. Then she licked him as he lay suffering in the snow. His brother licked him, too, as he whimpered with distress.

Finally the blood stopped, and after a long

time, the suffering stopped too. The cub sniffed the air and raised his head. His recovery began as he finally took the food he was offered.

Pain went away from her heart.

Before them lay all the arctic lands, the snow in retreat. The huge sheets of ice, warmed by the sun, were being broken up by the waves. Plant life teemed in the water. Millions of wildflowers dotted the rocky shore. There was everything to eat at once—moss and roots and fish and seals. Salmon and cod swam in the green water. Seaweed washed around the rocks. On the land there were rabbits and young birds.

And the mother bear, in the snow with her cubs, did not know why she behaved as she did. She only knew that there was pain and there was happiness. These two things drove her according to laws she did not understand. But when the summer ended and the polar night began, she would do the same things over again. And her children after her would do them too.

SELECTING DETAILS FROM THE STORY.
The following questions help you check your reading comprehension. Put an *x* in the box next to each correct answer.

1. The polar bear was fattening herself up because she
   - ☐ a. had lost weight recently due to sickness.
   - ☐ b. needed to store food for the cubs she was expecting.
   - ☐ c. wanted to be much bigger than her enemies.

2. Seal meat was the bear's favorite food because it was
   - ☐ a. tasty and warm.
   - ☐ b. crisp and cold.
   - ☐ c. not too tough.

3. The polar bear taught her cubs how to
   - ☐ a. build a den in the snow.
   - ☐ b. fish and kill.
   - ☐ c. make friends with the land-seals.

4. The wounded cub eventually
   - ☐ a. died as a result of his injuries.
   - ☐ b. was deserted by his mother.
   - ☐ c. recovered.

KNOWING NEW VOCABULARY WORDS.
The following questions check your vocabulary skills. Put an *x* in the box next to each correct answer.

1. Under the dark sky on the white land, the bear was part of the lonely, desolate landscape. As used here, the word *desolate* means
   - ☐ a. deserted.
   - ☐ b. popular.
   - ☐ c. frantic.

2. For a long time, the bear prepared herself for the difficult ordeal ahead. Which of the following best defines the word *ordeal*?
   - ☐ a. safety or shelter
   - ☐ b. a kind of food
   - ☐ c. a harsh experience

3. The polar bear felt a tremor of pain, and then the first cub was born. A *tremor* is
   - ☐ a. an announcement.
   - ☐ b. a shaking or trembling.
   - ☐ c. a dream.

4. She felt better as the pain diminished and faded away. The word *diminished* means
   - ☐ a. increased.
   - ☐ b. decreased.
   - ☐ c. revealed.

☐ × 5 = ☐

NUMBER
CORRECT

YOUR
SCORE

☐ × 5 = ☐

NUMBER
CORRECT

YOUR
SCORE

IDENTIFYING STORY ELEMENTS. The following questions check your knowledge of story elements. Put an *x* in the box next to each correct answer.

1. "Polar Night" is *set*
   - ☐ a. on an island in the Pacific Ocean.
   - ☐ b. in the arctic region.
   - ☐ c. in a zoo somewhere in Alaska.

2. Which statement best *characterizes* the polar bear?
   - ☐ a. Above all, she was concerned about the survival and welfare of her cubs.
   - ☐ b. She was willing to take many risks because she felt that life was unimportant.
   - ☐ c. Considering her size and strength, she was not very brave.

3. What happened last in the *plot* of the story?
   - ☐ a. The polar bear chose the place for her den.
   - ☐ b. The bear charged at her enemies who turned and ran.
   - ☐ c. The second cub was born.

4. What is true of the *style* of "Polar Night"?
   - ☐ a. There is no conflict anywhere in the story.
   - ☐ b. The story contains no descriptive passages.
   - ☐ c. There is no dialogue in the story.

LOOKING AT CLOZE. The following questions use the cloze technique to check your reading comprehension. Complete the paragraph by filling in each blank with one of the words listed below. Each word appears in the story. Since there are five words and four blanks, one of the words will not be used.

The polar bear's thick, warm coat of fur does more than _____ the bear from the freezing cold it must endure. The white coat also serves to camouflage, or conceal, the bear from its _____.
Against the _____ of snow and ice, the polar bear is very difficult to see. This permits the bear to _____ and surprise its unsuspecting prey.

essential   approach

landscape

protect   enemies

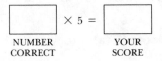

NUMBER CORRECT   × 5 =   YOUR SCORE

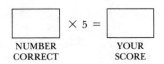

NUMBER CORRECT   × 5 =   YOUR SCORE

43

LEARNING HOW TO READ CRITICALLY.
The following questions check your critical thinking skills. Put an *x* in the box next to each correct answer.

1. What makes this story unusual is that the
   - ☐ a. plot is very complicated and hard to follow.
   - ☐ b. vocabulary is extremely difficult to understand.
   - ☐ c. main character is a polar bear.

2. When the bear saw the approaching men, she "thought about whether or not to kill them. But the unborn life in her said get away. So she dived and swam out of their range." This means that the bear
   - ☐ a. didn't want to place her unborn cubs in danger.
   - ☐ b. decided that the men weren't so bad after all.
   - ☐ c. didn't know if the men were armed.

3. There was an explosion and then "one cub gasped and doubled up as he was hit." We may infer that
   - ☐ a. a piece of ice snapped off an iceberg and struck the cub.
   - ☐ b. a large rock fell on the cub.
   - ☐ c. the cub had been shot.

4. Pain and happiness drove the bear "according to laws she did not understand." What laws are these?
   - ☐ a. the laws that govern the region
   - ☐ b. the laws of nature
   - ☐ c. the laws of supply and demand

	× 5 =	
NUMBER CORRECT		YOUR SCORE

Improving Writing and Discussion Skills

- "Polar Night" is a tale of struggle and survival. Find evidence from the story to support this statement. Show that the bear was well equipped to handle her environment.
- When the bear saw the men walking along the shore, she thought of them as "rare creatures and dangerous, even though they were so weak." Explain why she considered the men rare, dangerous, and weak.
- At one point during the story, the bear turned to meet her enemies, reared up, and galloped toward them in "a charge that nothing could stop—not even death. . . ." Suppose that you were with the hunters at the time. Describe the scene as vividly as you can.

Use the boxes below to total your scores for the exercises. Then write your score on pages 135 and 136.

☐ +	**S**ELECTING DETAILS FROM THE STOR
☐ +	**K**NOWING NEW VOCABULARY WORDS
☐ +	**I**DENTIFYING STORY ELEMENTS
☐ +	**L**OOKING AT CLOZE
☐ ▼	**L**EARNING HOW TO READ CRITICALL
☐	**S**core Total: Story 4

5. I'll Give You Law

by Molly Picon

Meet the Author
Molly Picon (1898–1992) was born
in New York and gained fame as an actress,
appearing in dozens of theatrical performances
in London, Paris, and on Broadway. She also
appeared in motion pictures and on radio and
TV programs. In addition to composing songs
and writing character sketches, Picon wrote
Molly! An Autobiography and *So Laugh a Little*,
in which "I'll Give You Law" appears.

*W*hen I read the newspaper, there is always a must section in it that I never pass by. This is the lost and found advertisements usually buried in the back pages. This is a habit I picked up from my grandmother. She always took a keen interest in who had lost what, and who was honestly reporting on items found.

We thought about all the lost items with equal interest. We wondered about the found items as well, visualizing the happy claimants, and the honest finders handsomely rewarded.

And then one day, we moved swiftly from the land of fantasy to a world of realities. My grandmother found something!

"What is it? What is it?" I asked, hopping with excitement.

"A lavaliere!"[1] My grandmother was absolutely overwhelmed. She had never found anything in her life, and now, here in her hand, was this magnificent lavaliere.

---

1. **lavaliere:** a piece of jewelry on a chain, worn as a necklace.

"It must be very expensive," I said, running my fingers over it.

"A fortune," my grandmother said positively. She held it up against her. "A regular fortune," she breathed.

"Are you going to keep it?" I asked.

She gave me a sharp look.

"Am I going to keep it?" she asked. "Such a question." She threw her shawl over her head.

"Where are you going?" I asked. "Can I go, too?"

"I'm going to the police station. Let them worry about it."

At the police station, the property clerk informed her politely that if the lavaliere was not claimed within ninety days, the police department would turn the jewelry over to her, and she would be its rightful and legal owner. He took her name and address and wrote it down. They would let her know, he said indifferently.

"Oh, I hope nobody claims it," I said fervently. "Oh, Grandma, I hope whoever lost it doesn't even know they lost it."

Such a dilemma for my grandmother. If ever she yearned for anything, it was for this lavaliere. On the other hand, her active imagination conjured up for her such fearful scenes that she couldn't wait for the loser to come and claim her property.

Meanwhile, my grandmother took to haunting the police station and the property clerk. "How are you," she would ask, "and how is the family?" When he would look up and see my grandmother, he would mutter and groan.

"Mrs. Ostrow," he would say, "don't you have anything to do at home?"

"Why don't I have something to do at home?" My grandmother would regard him scornfully. "You think I like to come here day after day?"

"So why do you come?" he would ask logically.

"To see what I have to see," she would tell him. And then she would demand to see the lavaliere with "my own eyes." And then she would subject him to a searching questioning. Who has come today, and what had they claimed, and wasn't it possible the lavaliere had belonged to one of the people who had come, and had he told anybody about it, and if he was keeping it such a big secret, how could anybody know he had it in the first place?

"Ninety days," he would cry, clutching his hair. "I'll never survive it."

I never knew that ninety days could last so long. But eventually the ninetieth day arrived, bringing with it much excitement. My grandmother and I dressed as though we were going to a party. She was going to allow me to go with her for the presentation. On the way we discussed her immense good fortune.

"When I die," she said to me, "I want you to have it."

"Please, Grandma," I said, uncomfortably. It seemed like a grim note to inject in an otherwise cloudless day.

"No," she insisted seriously. "I want you to have it. It will be like a—what is the word I want, Molly?"

"An heirloom?"

"That's the word." She pounced on it with satisfaction. "And when you die, your children will have it."

In two sentences, my grandmother had disposed of us both.

At the police station, my grandmother was greeted with happy smiles, even from the property clerk. I should say, especially from the property clerk.

When my grandmother finally held the lavaliere in her hand, her eyes misted over. She couldn't speak, but she nodded her head.

"Don't be a stranger," they urged her. "Don't wait till you find something before you drop in."

When we got home, my grandmother promptly put the lavaliere on.

"I'll wear it night and day," she vowed. "I'll never take it off." For a week she was as good as her word.

Then one day there came a knock at the door, and tragedy swept in, escorted by an embarrassed property clerk from the police station.

"Where is it?" cried the woman he had brought to the door. She looked at my grandmother. "My lavaliere she's wearing," she cried in horror, pointing to my grandmother.

My grandmother looked at both of them, shocked. Her hand went up automatically to clutch the lavaliere.

"It's mine," she said. "You told me, after ninety days . . ."

"That's right," the property clerk said promptly. "Legally it is yours. That's what I've been trying to tell this lady. She didn't claim it in ninety days and the law says . . ."

"I'll give you law," the lady shouted vigorously, pounding him on the arm. "Does the law say that after ninety days thieves and murderers can do whatever they want? Law! I'll give you law!"

"Please, lady," the property clerk pleaded. "Let's try to be calm."

"Calm!" she took up the cry. "I'll give you calm!"

My grandmother entered the fray briskly.

"So much commotion," she said. "You want the neighbors to think we're killing you on the doorstep. Come inside." She urged them in and closed the door. "So if you'll stop talking and tell me where you were," she said, guiding the distracted woman to a seat, "we'll listen and we'll be the same good friends."

"Where was I?" the woman said, shaking her head. "My daughter was having her baby, so she says to me, 'Ma,' she says, 'if you don't come, I won't have it, that's all.'

"So I had to go to Scranton. One month in advance, just in case. And then, the baby comes. Now she's afraid to hold it, it might break. And she's afraid to wash it. It might come apart in the water. One month. Two months. Finally I say to her, 'Enough is enough already. Whatever you'll do, you'll do.' "

My grandmother was already making tea for everybody, bustling about the kitchen, putting crackers and jam on the table.

"The young people today," she commented.

"So when I come back, I first realized my lavaliere is gone. I'm not hung with jewelry, and between you and me and the lamppost," she added confidentially to my grandmother, "I need a lavaliere like I need a hole in the head. But when I need a little extra money in an emergency, that lavaliere saves my life."

"How does it save your life?" I asked.

"I bring it to the pawnshop and whatever he gives me . . ."

"The pawnshop!" I was indignant. "She doesn't even wear it, Grandma," I said passionately. "Don't give it back. You don't have to. The law says you don't have to."

"That's right," the property clerk said instantly. He was on his second cup of tea and using my grandmother's jam as if the jar had an endless bottom.

The woman opened her mouth to protest, but my grandmother stopped her by holding up her hand for silence.

"Molly," she said gently, "there is a law here, too." She laid her hand tenderly on my heart: "Look in your heart and tell me. Suppose it was your lavaliere. Suppose you lost it and somebody else found it. Ninety days, a thousand days . . . how would you feel?"

"I would want it back," I answered honestly.

She spread her hands out eloquently. "So?" she asked me.

"That's not fair," I burst out.

"Fair? Who said anything about fair?" She reached up and took off the lavaliere. She fondled it for a moment, and then handed it over to the woman.

"Why should I complain?" she asked no one in particular and shrugged. "For three months I lived in a dream, and for five days I lived like a queen. Is that bad?"

SELECTING DETAILS FROM THE STORY.
The following questions help you check your
reading comprehension. Put an *x* in the box
next to each correct answer.

1. According to the property clerk, the
   lavaliere would legally belong to
   Mrs. Ostrow if it was not claimed within
   ☐ a. two weeks.
   ☐ b. a month.
   ☐ c. ninety days.

2. Mrs. Ostrow said that when she died, the
   lavaliere would go to
   ☐ a. Molly.
   ☐ b. the person who lost it.
   ☐ c. charity.

3. The woman who lost the lavaliere didn't
   claim it earlier because she
   ☐ a. was wealthy and didn't need it until
   recently.
   ☐ b. had been away helping her daughter
   and didn't realize it was missing.
   ☐ c. was on vacation out of the country
   and had just returned home.

4. While the property clerk was waiting at
   Mrs. Ostrow's house, he
   ☐ a. tried to convince Mrs. Ostrow to
   return the lavaliere.
   ☐ b. threatened to throw the other woman
   in jail for creating a disturbance.
   ☐ c. had two cups of tea and some jam.

KNOWING NEW VOCABULARY WORDS. The
following questions check your vocabulary
skills. Put an *x* in the box next to each correct
answer.

1. They thought about lost items that had
   been returned, visualizing the happy
   people who were glad to have their articles
   again. The word *visualizing* means
   ☐ a. picturing.
   ☐ b. blaming.
   ☐ c. asking.

2. This was her dilemma: On the one hand
   she yeared to keep the lavaliere, but at
   the same time she couldn't wait to return
   it. A *dilemma* is a situation that
   ☐ a. is very easy to solve.
   ☐ b. usually brings a person riches.
   ☐ c. requires one to make a difficult
   choice.

3. "Oh, I hope nobody claims it," Molly
   exclaimed fervently. What is the meaning
   of the word *fervently*?
   ☐ a. weakly
   ☐ b. earnestly
   ☐ c. sadly

4. The woman shouted at the property clerk
   and pounded him on the arm until
   Mrs. Ostrow entered the fray. A *fray* is a
   ☐ a. noisy quarrel.
   ☐ b. police station.
   ☐ c. tray of refreshments.

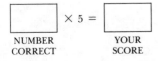

NUMBER   YOUR
CORRECT   SCORE

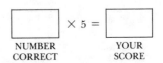

NUMBER   YOUR
CORRECT   SCORE

IDENTIFYING STORY ELEMENTS. The following questions check your knowledge of story elements. Put an *x* in the box next to each correct answer.

1. Who is the *narrator* of "I'll Give You Law?"?
   - ☐ a. Molly
   - ☐ b. the grandmother
   - ☐ c. the property clerk

2. What happened first in the *plot* of the story?
   - ☐ a. Molly urged her grandmother not to give back the lavaliere.
   - ☐ b. A woman claimed that Mrs. Ostrow was wearing her lavaliere.
   - ☐ c. Mrs. Ostrow took the lavaliere to the police station.

3. Which pair of words best *characterizes* Mrs. Ostrow?
   - ☐ a. honest; caring
   - ☐ b. greedy; stubborn
   - ☐ c. boastful; dishonest

4. Identify the statement that illustrates *inner conflict*.
   - ☐ a. Although Mrs. Ostrow didn't have a lot of money, she acted generously.
   - ☐ b. Although Mrs. Ostrow wanted to keep the lavaliere, she felt it rightfully belonged to the person who lost it.
   - ☐ c. Although Mrs. Ostrow knew that the lavaliere was valuable, she didn't think it was particularly attractive.

LOOKING AT CLOZE. The following questions use the cloze technique to check your reading comprehension. Complete the paragraph by filling in each blank with one of the words listed below. Each word appears in the story. Since there are five words and four blanks, one of the words will not be used.

"The _____ has its reasons
                1

which reason knows nothing of." More than

three hundred years ago, a French philosopher,

Blaise Pascal, _____ those
                            2

words. They suggest that *feelings* rather

than reason or _____ often
                          3

govern our actions—and that we do not

_____ this, or care to, when
              4

we act as we do.

heart   realize

magnificent

logic   wrote

	× 5 =	
NUMBER CORRECT		YOUR SCORE

	× 5 =	
NUMBER CORRECT		YOUR SCORE

LEARNING HOW TO READ CRITICALLY.
The following questions check your critical
thinking skills. Put an *x* in the box next to
each correct answer.

1. Evidence in the story suggests that
   Mrs. Ostrow returned the lavaliere
   because she
   ☐ a. didn't want to break the law.
   ☐ b. was afraid of the woman who lost it.
   ☐ c. knew in her heart it was the right
   thing to do.

2. Which statement is true?
   ☐ a. When the woman claimed the
   lavaliere, Mrs. Ostrow grew angry.
   ☐ b. Mrs. Ostrow appeared at the police
   station so often, the police
   considered her a nuisance at first.
   ☐ c. When Mrs. Ostrow decided to return
   the lavaliere, Molly was very pleased.

3. Story clues indicate that the woman
   needed the lavaliere
   ☐ a. in order to borrow money from time
   to time.
   ☐ b. to wear on formal occasions.
   ☐ c. to impress her friends.

4. Had the woman claimed the lavaliere a
   year later than she did, it is likely that
   Mrs. Ostrow would have
   ☐ a. laughed at the woman and told her
   to leave.
   ☐ b. said that she needed time to decide
   what to do.
   ☐ c. given back the lavaliere.

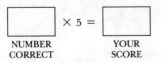

NUMBER
CORRECT

YOUR
SCORE

Improving Writing and Discussion Skills

- At the conclusion of the story
  Mrs. Ostrow said, "For three months
  I lived in a dream, and for five
  days I lived like a queen." What did
  Mrs. Ostrow mean by that statement?
- "There is a law here, too," explained
  Mrs. Ostrow, referring to the heart.
  What law is that? Do you think that
  the property clerk was surprised when
  Mrs. Ostrow returned the piece of
  jewelry? Why?
- When Molly wrote the story, do you
  think she was proud of her grand-
  mother, or did she consider her foolish?
  Give reasons to support your opinion.

Use the boxes below to total your scores
for the exercises. Then write your score on
pages 135 and 136.

SELECTING DETAILS FROM THE STORY

+

KNOWING NEW VOCABULARY WORDS

+

IDENTIFYING STORY ELEMENTS

+

LOOKING AT CLOZE

+

LEARNING HOW TO READ CRITICALLY

▼

Score Total: Story 5

6. **A Habit for the Voyage**

by Robert Edmond Alter

$\mathcal{T}$he moment Kreuger stepped aboard the ship, he sensed that something was wrong. He had never really understood these warnings, but he had had them before, and usually he had been right.

He paused on the gangplank and looked around. He could see the deckhands loading the last of the cargo aboard. The steward was standing about twenty feet ahead, with Kreuger's shabby suitcase in his hand. He looked back at Kreuger impatiently.

Kreuger took one final look around, saw nothing out of the ordinary, and stepped across the deck to follow the steward.

It came again—a sudden sense of danger—so sharply that he actually flinched. Then, as a black object went flying past his sight, he threw himself to one side. The object, whatever it was, smacked to the deck right at his feet with a thudding crash.

Kreuger took one glance at it—a metal bucket filled to the top with nails and screws. He stepped quickly to his right and thrust his hand under his raincoat to get at the

Meet the Author

Robert Edmond Alter (1925–1965) was born in San Francisco, where he worked at a variety of jobs before devoting himself full time to writing. He is the author of more than two hundred short stories and seventeen novels, several of which have won Gold Medal awards. His writing is highly original and, as "A Habit for the Voyage" suggests, is often filled with danger and suspense.

pistol in his right-hand pocket. Then he stared upward at the shadowy deck above him and to the railing on the deck above that.

Kreuger couldn't see anything. Nothing moved up there.

The steward was coming back toward him, a look of shock on his face. "What happened?" he called.

Kreuger quickly withdrew his empty hand from under his coat. He realized that the incident had drawn attention.

"Some fool nearly killed me with that bucket—that's what!"

The steward looked at the bucket, still half full. "Those deckhands," he remarked, "are careless fellows."

Kreuger was getting back his breath. The steward was right, he thought to himself. It had been an accident, of course. "Please show me to my cabin," he said softly.

The steward nodded and led him down a poorly lit corridor to his stateroom. It was on the starboard side, in the second-class section, and it wasn't very large. It contained a porthole, a sink, a closet, and a bunk. That was all.

Kreuger was careful to give the steward a modest tip. Then he seated himself on the bunk with a sigh, as though prepared to relax and enjoy his trip. Kreuger always tried to maintain a mild, bland air in front of people who served him. It was one of his rules: never do anything that makes you stand out. Stewards, waiters, and desk clerks had an annoying way of being able to remember certain *mannerisms*—habits or traits—about you, when questioned later.

The steward thanked Kreuger and left the room. For a moment, Kreuger stayed where he was. Then he got up and went over to lock the door. He opened his suitcase, took out

a roll of adhesive tape, and cut four eight-inch strips. Then, getting down on his knees, he placed his pistol underneath the sink and taped it there. Just a precaution—in case someone went through his things when he was out of the room.

Kreuger never relied on a firearm for his work. It was messy and much too obvious. No, he was a man who arranged innocent-looking *accidents*. The pistol was a weapon he used only in self-defense—in case there was a hitch and he was forced to fight his way out. This had happened more than once during his career. For Kreuger was what is known in the trade as a secret agent. He was one of the best. Among other things, he knew seven languages and felt completely comfortable speaking any one of them. That was important in his business.

Kreuger sat back in his bunk and thought for a while about the man, the man aboard this ship—the man he was going to do away with.

Unconsciously, Kreuger brought his right hand up to his ear and began to tug gently at the lobe. When he caught himself doing this, he hurriedly snatched his hand away. That was a *bad habit* with him—one that he had to watch. Bad habits were dangerous in his business. Exceedingly dangerous. They gave away your identity. They gave an enemy agent a chance to spot you. It was like walking around in public wearing a sign that said: *I am Kreuger. I am Kreuger, the Secret Agent.*

He remembered only too well what had happened to his old friend, Delchev. Delchev had developed a bad habit—of occasionally pulling at his tie. Over the years, the word had gotten around. The habit had been noted and recorded. It went into all the enemy files and folders on Delchev. Delchev was identified by his habit. And no matter what alias or disguise he used, sooner or later it gave him away. In the end, it had cost him his life.

Kreuger had known of another agent who liked to break toothpicks in half. He was dead now too.

And there was one fellow who used so many different disguises, he was simply referred to by those in the business as Mr. D. Kreuger believed that he could have tracked down Mr. D. within six months, had someone made it worth his while, because there was a note in the file on Mr. D—of a bad habit, one that identified him. Mr. D. always revealed himself by scratching a paper matchbook with his thumbnail.

Well, at least tugging at your ear wasn't that bad. Not as bad as scratching a matchbook with your thumbnail. But it was bad enough and Kreuger knew it. He must be more careful about his habits in the future. He had to weed out anything that could give him away.

The distant clang of a ship's bell reached him. Dinnertime.

All right. Time to go to work, to proceed. Time to view the future victim.

In the dining room, Kreuger looked around, found the table he wanted, and sat down. The room seemed to him dull and dingy. This suggested that the food would be poorly prepared. But Kreuger knew in advance that he would say nothing. Never call attention to yourself by being a complainer.

He picked up a napkin and started to tuck it into his collar. Then he caught himself in time and put it on his lap instead.

Watch it! Watch that sort of thing. You put your napkin in your collar on your last assignment. Never repeat the same mannerism twice in a row!

Kreuger smiled at the man across the table and said, "If you don't mind, pass the menu, please."

The man Kreuger addressed was a harmless-looking, slender little fellow of about forty, with thinning hair and glasses. His name was Amos Bicker—and he was the man slated for a fatal accident—one arranged by Kreuger.

While he pretended to examine the menu, Kreuger secretly studied his intended victim. He certainly didn't look like the sort who needed killing. However, Kreuger's instructions were quite clear. So be it then. Now for the means to accomplish the . . .

Kreuger caught his hand halfway to his ear. *Blast it!* He continued the gesture but scratched the back of his neck. He put the menu down and ordered oysters for an appetizer. Then, turning to the woman on his left, he began speaking to her in Spanish, which she understood. All the time, however, he was thinking about the man across the table—Bicker—and wondering how to dispose of him.

Kreuger always preferred obvious accidents. Therefore, when aboard a ship, man overboard. This could be accomplished in a variety of ways. The simplest was to make friends with the victim, then arrange an evening stroll along the deck. A sudden, sharp push would achieve the goal. Man overboard.

The waiter brought Kreuger his oysters. As Kreuger reached for his fork, he gave a start. Something was brushing against his leg under the table. He leaned back in his chair and raised the cloth. A scruffy-looking old cat—the ship's cat, probably—was standing there.

"Here, kitty, kitty," Kreuger said. He loved animals. Had he led a quieter, more peaceful life, he would have had a home, and the home would have been filled with pets. He'd have been married too.

A ship's officer appeared in the doorway. "Who is Señor Werfel?" he called into the room.

"Here!" Kreuger replied. That was one thing he never slipped up on. He could pick up and drop an alias with the snap of his fingers. And on this voyage, he had signed on as Señor Werfel.

"The captain wishes to see you for a moment, señor."

The word *why* flashed into Kreuger's brain. Then he found the obvious answer and stood up, smiling. The incident with the bucket, no doubt. This was annoying because it called further attention to him. However there was really nothing that he could do.

Moments later Kreuger met the captain on the bridge of the ship. There, the captain repeatedly apologized for the unfortunate accident. Kreuger laughed it off. "It was really nothing, Captain," he said. "I wish that you would put it out of your mind." He shook the captain's hand and returned at once to the dining room.

But something had happened during his absence.

Passengers were crowded around a space near his table. Kreuger could see that the cook and the waiter were attending to something on the floor. It was the ship's cat, and it was stretched out and lying there silently.

"*Oh*, Mr. Werfel," said the lady who had been seated next to Kreuger, "I did a *terrible* thing. No, come to think of it, it was fortunate that I did. Certainly fortunate for *you!*"

"What?" Kreuger said sharply, his eyes fixed on the cat. "What did you do?"

"That *poor* little dear jumped up on your seat after you left. He wanted your oysters.

Of course I held him off, but you were so long in returning. . . ."

"You gave him the oysters I ordered," said Kreuger.

"Yes! I finally did. And before any of us knew it, the poor thing began to shake terribly—and then it was gone."

"I better take care of this," said the ship's doctor, who had arrived on the scene.

Kreuger waited until the passengers had thinned out, then he took the waiter aside. "What was wrong with those oysters?" he demanded.

The waiter seemed utterly astonished. "I don't know. Perhaps ptomaine.[1] They were canned, of course."

"Let's see the can," said Kreuger.

There was a faint, unpleasant scent to the can, one able to be detected if held close to the nose.

Kreuger put down the can and looked at the waiter.

"Anyone else order oysters?"

"No, señor. Only yourself."

Kreuger forced a smile. "Well, accidents will happen," he said. But he certainly wished there were some way he could have analyzed the contents of that can. He returned to his room more angry than shaken.

Well, that had been close. Very close. *Too* close. But no matter how you looked at it, he had been very lucky. Of course it *could* have been ptomaine . . . food poisoning sometimes happened . . . but when you combined it with the business about the bucket—

He went to the sink and reached under for his gun.

---

1. **ptomaine:** a sometimes poisonous chemical, produced by bacteria in food that has not been properly canned.

It wasn't there! The tape was there, neatly, but not the pistol.

Now wait, he warned himself, tugging at his ear. A sailor *could* have kicked over the bucket by accident. Ptomaine poisoning *does* occur in carelessly canned meats. And things *are* sometimes stolen from compartments . . .

But the combination still spelled suspicion. Yet even if his suspicions were right, what could he do? He couldn't prove that the bucket and the food poisoning weren't accidents. He couldn't reveal that he'd brought a loaded pistol aboard.

I must tread very carefully, he thought. Very, very carefully, until this business is over. Tugging furiously at his ear, he read for a while. Then he undressed, turned out the light, and got into his bunk.

At first he thought it must be the wool blanket that was scratching him. Then he remembered that there was a sheet between his body and the blanket. Then he was certain that it wasn't the blanket—because it seemed to be moving.

He felt something fuzzy on his bare chest, something crawling sluggishly under the blanket. Kreuger started to raise the edge of the blanket, and the thing—whatever it was—scrambled onto his stomach. He froze, sucking in his breath, too scared to move a muscle.

It stopped, too, as if waiting for the man to make the first move. He could feel it there, on his bare skin, squatting, poised and waiting. He could feel the tiny feet advancing toward his rib cage.

He'd had it. Coordinating his movements, he threw the blanket and sheet aside with his left hand, as he swung his right arm across his stomach. Then he rolled off the bunk to the floor.

He was up instantly and frantically fumbling for the light switch.

The thing scurried across the sheet—a thick-legged, deadly tarantula. Kreuger snatched up a shoe and with two sharp blows disposed of the spider.

He threw the shoe aside and went to the sink. There he washed the beads of perspiration from his face. There was no call button in his stateroom. He opened his door and shouted, "Steward!"

A few minutes later the steward, with a sleepy smile, looked in. "Yes, Señor Werfel?"

Silently, Kreuger pointed to the crushed spider on his bed. The steward looked at it, made a face, and grunted. But he didn't seem particularly surprised.

"It happens. It is from the cargo, señor. They come aboard in the bananas. Some of them sometimes find their way through the ship."

It was the kind of answer Kreuger had expected, a reasonable explanation that left no room for argument. But this was getting to be too much. The tarantula was the last straw.

"See if you can find me the captain," said Kreuger, flatly.

The steward shrugged. He was not eager to bother the captain at this time of night. Still . . .

"Never mind!" said Kreuger rudely, as he shoved by the steward. "I'll find him myself!" Kreuger paused and took a deep breath. He was starting to forget all his rules.

The captain was no help at all. He merely repeated all of his sad, tiresome excuses: clumsy deckhands, careless canning, the bothersome little hazards of taking on bananas as cargo.

"Now look here, Captain," said Kreuger, angrily pulling at his ear, "I'm a reasonable man, and I'll go along with everyday accidents as long as they stay within the limits of probability. But all of these accidents have happened to *me*. All within one day!"

"What is it that you're trying to say, Mr. Werfel? Surely you're not implying that someone aboard this ship is trying to kill you, are you? You're not suggesting that? You don't have enemies, do you?"

Kreuger balked at that. It was a subject he wanted to stay away from.

"I said no such thing, Captain! All I'm saying is that these things keep happening aboard your ship. And I expect you to offer some protection."

"Certainly, Mr. Werfel. Let me see. Yes . . . I can give you your choice of any of my officers' cabins, if you like, my own included. I can assign a competent officer to stay by your side and—"

"No, no, no!" Kreuger said, hastily. "That isn't at all necessary, Captain. I don't intend to act like a prisoner aboard this ship!"

Turning angrily on his heels, Kreuger began to make his way back to his stateroom. He needed to relax, to think. His nerves were getting out of hand and no wonder! The whole game was going very badly, turning sour on him. He was calling attention to himself and . . .

He paused on the passageway that overlooked the dark deck below. Someone was down there on the deck, someone familiar, leaning over the low rail, staring out to the sea.

Kreuger ran his hand over his face, wiping away the sea mist there. Slowly he walked down the steps . . . quietly, ever so quietly.

The man on the deck was Amos Bicker. He was looking out at the black, rambling sea, his elbows up on the rail, his thin back to Kreuger.

Kreuger quietly came down another step. His eyes quickly checked out everything with professional interest.

Bicker was leaning over the low railing. Below him was nothing—nothing except the open sea.

Made to order! Kreuger could finish his business here and now. Then he could concentrate on his own survival, guard himself against those recurring accidents— if accidents, indeed, were what they were.

Kreuger came down the last step. He planted both feet on the deck. He looked around once more. Kreuger and the victim were the only ones there—and the unsuspecting victim thought that he was alone!

It wouldn't take much—just a short, sudden run and a shove—to thrust Bicker over the rail and into the sea.

Kreuger smiled a tight grin. Then he broke into an eager, cat-footed run.

All the lifeboats had returned and the captain had received their reports. Shaking his head sadly, he entered his office and sat down at the seat behind the desk.

"Well," he said, "this is certainly a sorry business. Unfortunate that you had to be involved in it, Mr. Bicker."

Amos Bicker was sitting bent over in his chair facing the desk. His nerves were obviously in a bad state. His hands trembled, his voice trembled too.

"You didn't recover the—uh—"

"Not a sign of the body," the captain said. "He must have gone down like a stone. But please, Mr. Bicker, please do not let it prey on your mind. You couldn't have done more than you did. You called *man overboard* the moment it happened. You did all you could."

Mr. Bicker shivered, and the captain thought that he might be going into shock.

"He must have been mad—crazy," Bicker said, finally. "I didn't know the man, had never seen him, except in the dining room this evening. I was just standing there at the rail minding my own business, watching the sea without a thought in my head. And then I heard a—a movement, a sort of quiet rushing motion, and I looked around and there he was. Coming right at me! And the look on his face!"

"Yes, yes, Mr. Bicker," the captain said sympathetically. "We quite understand. There's no doubt in anyone's mind that there was something—well, odd in Mr. Werfel's behavior. I have reason to believe that he actually thought that someone aboard the ship was trying to kill him. Strange fellow. Lucky for you that you stepped aside at the last minute—or he might have taken you over the side with him."

Mr. Bicker stared at the carpet and nodded. One of his thumbnails was idly scratching the edge of a paper matchbook.

SELECTING DETAILS FROM THE STORY.
The following questions help you check your
reading comprehension. Put an *x* in the box
next to each correct answer.

1. When Kreuger stepped aboard the ship,
   he was nearly killed by a
   - ☐ a. deckhand who tried to push him
     overboard.
   - ☐ b. deadly spider.
   - ☐ c. heavy bucket that went flying past
     his head.

2. Kreuger's bad habit was that he would
   - ☐ a. tug at his ear.
   - ☐ b. break toothpicks in half.
   - ☐ c. scratch paper matchbooks with his
     thumbnail.

3. Kreuger's favorite way of disposing of a
   victim was by
   - ☐ a. using a firearm.
   - ☐ b. arranging an innocent-looking
     "accident."
   - ☐ c. poisoning the unsuspecting person.

4. According to the captain, Mr. Werfel
   was a
   - ☐ a. typical passenger.
   - ☐ b. secret agent in disguise.
   - ☐ c. strange fellow whose behavior
     was odd.

KNOWING NEW VOCABULARY WORDS. The
following questions check your vocabulary
skills. Put an *x* in the box next to each correct
answer.

1. Kreuger felt the sense of danger so sharply
   that he actually flinched. What is the
   meaning of the word *flinched*?
   - ☐ a. laughed loudly.
   - ☐ b. drew back.
   - ☐ c. surrendered.

2. Since he didn't want to stand out or be
   remembered, Kreuger always maintained
   a mild, bland air. The word *bland* means
   - ☐ a. loud and demanding.
   - ☐ b. terrified or frightening.
   - ☐ c. gentle and soothing.

3. Amos Bicker was the man slated for a fatal
   accident—one arranged by Kreuger. As
   used here, the word *slated* means
   - ☐ a. scheduled or listed.
   - ☐ b. applauded or cheered.
   - ☐ c. bothered or annoyed.

4. "You're not implying that someone aboard
   this ship is trying to kill you, are you?
   You're not suggesting that?" said the
   captain. Define the word *implying*.
   - ☐ a. hinting
   - ☐ b. attacking
   - ☐ c. avoiding

☐ × 5 = ☐

NUMBER CORRECT   YOUR SCORE

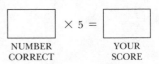

☐ × 5 = ☐

NUMBER CORRECT   YOUR SCORE

IDENTIFYING STORY ELEMENTS. The following questions check your knowledge of story elements. Put an *x* in the box next to each correct answer.

1. "A Habit for the Voyage" is *set* on
   - ☐ a. a train.
   - ☐ b. a ship.
   - ☐ c. an island in South America.

2. Which statement *characterizes* both Kreuger and Mr. D.?
   - ☐ a. Each had the habit of tugging at his tie.
   - ☐ b. Each was married and lived a quiet, peaceful life.
   - ☐ c. Each was a secret agent who used various aliases.

3. What happened last in the *plot* of the story?
   - ☐ a. Kreuger grinned and then rushed at Amos Bicker.
   - ☐ b. Passengers crowded around the cat that was lying on the floor.
   - ☐ c. Kreuger felt something crawling on his chest.

4. The *mood* of "A Habit for the Voyage" is
   - ☐ a. humorous.
   - ☐ b. suspenseful.
   - ☐ c. joyous.

LOOKING AT CLOZE. The following questions use the cloze technique to check your reading comprehension. Complete the paragraph by filling in each blank with one of the words listed below. Each word appears in the story. Since there are five words and four blanks, one of the words will not be used.

Dozens of things that you do every day are done by _____ . For example,
     1
when you enter an elevator you automatically

_____ out and press a button.
     2
You know, by habit, to stop at a red signal

and to _____ on the green. Life
     3
would be impossibly difficult, indeed, if we

had to learn over and over what we already

_____ know by habit.
     4

proceed   habit

unconsciously

reach   victim

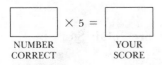

NUMBER   YOUR
CORRECT   SCORE

☐ × 5 = ☐

NUMBER   YOUR
CORRECT   SCORE

61

LEARNING HOW TO READ CRITICALLY.
The following questions check your critical
thinking skills. Put an *x* in the box next to
each correct answer.

1. The last paragraph of the story leads the
   reader to
   ☐ a. feel sorry for Amos Bicker.
   ☐ b. wonder if Kreuger is still alive.
   ☐ c. realize that Amos Bicker is Mr. D.

2. We may infer that Amos Bicker
   ☐ a. was a harmless little fellow.
   ☐ b. planned and carried out the death
   of Kreuger.
   ☐ c. had no idea who Mr. Werfel was.

3. When he spoke rudely to the steward and
   shoved past him, Kreuger realized that
   he was "starting to forget all his rules."
   What rules had Kreuger forgotten?
   ☐ a. Never let anyone take advantage of
   you.
   ☐ b. Never do anything to call attention
   to yourself.
   ☐ c. Always keep a firearm nearby.

4. Bicker seemed so shaken by what happened at the rail, "the captain thought
   that he might be going into shock." Story
   clues indicate that Bicker
   ☐ a. wasn't upset at all but was merely
   acting.
   ☐ b. was stunned because a fellow
   passenger had fallen overboard.
   ☐ c. was nervous because he feared that
   the captain suspected him of a crime.

	× 5 =	
NUMBER CORRECT		YOUR SCORE

Improving Writing and Discussion Skills

• There are numerous encounters in
"A Habit for the Voyage." List as
many as you can. Then select one
and describe it in detail.
• Kreuger does not realize that there
is another assassin, or murderer,
aboard the ship. What clues should
have alerted Kreuger to the presence
of a clever and deadly enemy?
• Show that Mr. D. was truly a master
of disguise. Should Kreuger have
become suspicious when he saw
Amos Bicker leaning over the rail?
Explain.

Use the boxes below to total your scores
for the exercises. Then write your score on
pages 135 and 136.

☐ +	**S**ELECTING DETAILS FROM THE STOR
☐ +	**K**NOWING NEW VOCABULARY WORD:
☐ +	**I**DENTIFYING STORY ELEMENTS
☐ +	**L**OOKING AT CLOZE
☐ ▼	**L**EARNING HOW TO READ CRITICAL
☐	**S**core Total: Story 6

7. **Eleven**

by Sandra Cisneros

Meet the Author

Sandra Cisneros (1954–   ) taught English in high school and at various colleges before devoting herself full time to writing. Born in Chicago to Mexican-American parents, Cisneros grew up speaking both English and Spanish. An award-winning author, her works include *The House on Mango Street* and *Woman Hollering Creek* and the volumes of poetry, *My Wicked, Wicked Ways* and *Loose Woman*.

*W*hat they don't understand about birthdays and what they never tell you is that when you're eleven, you're also ten, and nine, and eight, and seven, and six, and five, and four, and three, and two, and one. And when you wake up on your eleventh birthday you expect to feel eleven, but you don't. You open your eyes and everything's just like yesterday, only it's today. And you don't feel eleven at all. You feel like you're still ten. And you are— underneath the year that makes you eleven.

Like some days you might say something stupid, and that's the part of you that's still ten. Or maybe some days you might need to sit on your mama's lap because you're scared, and that's the part of you that's five.

And maybe one day when you're all grown up maybe you will need to cry like if you're three, and that's okay. That's what I tell Mama when she's sad and needs to cry. Maybe she's feeling three.

Because the way you grow old is kind of like an onion or like the rings inside a tree trunk or like my little wooden dolls that fit one inside the other, each year inside the next one. That's how being eleven years old is.

You don't feel eleven. Not right away. It takes a few days, weeks even, sometimes even months before you say Eleven when they ask you. And you don't feel smart eleven, not until you're almost twelve. That's the way it is.

Only today I wish I didn't have only eleven years rattling inside me like pennies in a tin Band-Aid box. Today I wish I was one hundred and two instead of eleven because if I was one hundred and two I'd have known what to say when Mrs. Price put the red sweater on my desk. I would've known how to tell her it wasn't mine instead of just sitting there with that look on my face and nothing coming out of my mouth.

"Whose is this?" Mrs. Price says, and she holds the red sweater up in the air for all the class to see. "Whose? It's been sitting in the coatroom for a month."

"Not mine," says everybody. "Not me."

"It has to belong to somebody," Mrs. Price keeps saying, but nobody can remember. It's an ugly sweater with red plastic buttons and a collar and sleeves all stretched out like you could use it for a jump rope. It's maybe a thousand years old and even if it belonged to me I wouldn't say so.

Maybe because I'm skinny, maybe because she doesn't like me, that stupid Sylvia Saldívar says, "I think it belongs to Rachel." An ugly sweater like that, all raggedy and old, but

Mrs. Price believes her. Mrs. Price takes the sweater and puts it right on my desk, but when I open my mouth nothing comes out.

"That's not, I don't, you're not . . . Not mine," I finally say in a little voice that was maybe me when I was four.

"Of course it's yours," Mrs. Price says. "I remember you wearing it once." Because she's older and the teacher, she's right and I'm not.

Not mine, not mine, not mine, but Mrs. Price is already turning to page thirty-two, and math problem number four. I don't know why but all of a sudden I'm feeling sick inside, like the part of me that's three wants to come out of my eyes, only I squeeze them shut tight and bite down on my teeth real hard and try to remember today I am eleven, eleven. Mama is baking a cake for me tonight, and when Papa comes home everybody will sing Happy birthday, happy birthday to you.

But when the sick feeling goes away and I open my eyes, the red sweater's still sitting there like a big red mountain. I move the red sweater to the corner of my desk with my ruler. I move my pencil and books and eraser as far from it as possible. I even move my chair a little to the right. Not mine, not mine, not mine.

In my head I'm thinking how long till lunchtime, how long till I can take the red sweater and throw it over the schoolyard fence, or leave it hanging on a parking meter, or bunch it up into a little ball and toss it in the alley. Except when math period ends Mrs. Price says loud and in front of everybody, "Now, Rachel, that's enough," because she sees I've shoved the red sweater to the tippy-tip corner of my desk and it's hanging all over the edge like a waterfall, but I don't care.

"Rachel," Mrs. Price says. She says it like she's getting mad. "You put that sweater on right now and no more nonsense."

"But it's not—"

"Now!" Mrs. Price says.

This is when I wish I wasn't eleven, because all the years inside of me—ten, nine, eight, seven, six, five, four, three, two, and one—are pushing at the back of my eyes when I put one arm through one sleeve of the sweater that smells like cottage cheese, and then the other arm through the other and stand there with my arms apart like if the sweater hurts me and it does, all itchy and full of germs that aren't even mine.

That's when everything I've been holding in since this morning, since when Mrs. Price put the sweater on my desk, finally lets go, and all of a sudden I'm crying in front of everybody. I wish I was invisible but I'm not. I'm eleven and it's my birthday today and I'm crying like I'm three in front of everybody. I put my head down on the desk and bury my face in my stupid clown-sweater arms. My face all hot and spit coming out of my mouth because I can't stop the little animal noises from coming out of me, until there aren't any more tears left in my eyes, and it's just my body shaking like when you have the hiccups, and my whole head hurts like when you drink milk too fast.

But the worst part is right before the bell rings for lunch. That stupid Phyllis Lopez, who is even dumber than Sylvia Saldívar, says she remembers the red sweater is hers! I take it off right away and give it to her, only Mrs. Price pretends like everything's okay.

Today I'm eleven. There's a cake Mama's making for tonight, and when Papa comes home from work we'll eat it. There'll be candles and presents and everybody will sing Happy birthday, happy birthday to you, Rachel, only it's too late.

I'm eleven today. I'm eleven, ten, nine, eight, seven, six, five, four, three, two, and one, but I wish I was one hundred and two. I wish I was anything but eleven, because I want today to be far away already, far away like a runaway balloon, like a tiny *o* in the sky, so tiny-tiny you have to close your eyes to see it.

Selecting details from the story.

The following questions help you check your reading comprehension. Put an *x* in the box next to each correct answer.

1. Mrs. Price said that sweater had been in the coatroom for a
   - ☐ a. few days.
   - ☐ b. week.
   - ☐ c. month.

2. According to Rachel, the sweater was
   - ☐ a. fairly nice looking.
   - ☐ b. ugly, raggedy, and old.
   - ☐ c. red and new.

3. Mrs. Price gave the sweater to Rachel because
   - ☐ a. the teacher wanted Rachel to have it for a birthday present.
   - ☐ b. the teacher thought she saw Rachel wearing it earlier.
   - ☐ c. Rachel said that the sweater was hers.

4. After she put on the sweater, Rachel
   - ☐ a. burst into tears.
   - ☐ b. ran out into the hall.
   - ☐ c. smiled although she was feeling ill.

Knowing new vocabulary words.

The following questions check your vocabulary skills. Put an *x* in the box next to each correct answer.

1. Her body began shaking "like when you have the hiccups." When you have the *hiccups,* you
   - ☐ a. catch your breath as you make sharp, clicking sounds.
   - ☐ b. rest in bed with a terrible headache.
   - ☐ c. complain about a sore throat.

2. When Rachel began crying in front of everyone, she wished that she were invisible and put her head down on the desk and buried her face. The word *invisible* means
   - ☐ a. a great deal older.
   - ☐ b. very cheerful.
   - ☐ c. not able to be seen.

3. The sweater had red plastic buttons and very long sleeves. As used here, the word *plastic* means
   - ☐ a. an unusual color.
   - ☐ b. a kind of material.
   - ☐ c. many different prices.

4. She thought about leaving the sweater on a parking meter. Define the word *meter* as used in this sentence.
   - ☐ a. an instrument that records time
   - ☐ b. a shelf in a clothing store
   - ☐ c. the rhythm in a poem

	× 5 =	
NUMBER CORRECT		YOUR SCORE

	× 5 =	
NUMBER CORRECT		YOUR SCORE

IDENTIFYING STORY ELEMENTS. The following questions check your knowledge of story elements. Put an *x* in the box next to each correct answer.

1. Who is the *main character* in "Eleven"?
   - ☐ a. Rachel
   - ☐ b. Mrs. Price
   - ☐ c. Sylvia Saldívar

2. What happened last in the *plot* of the story?
   - ☐ a. Phyllis Lopez said that the sweater was hers.
   - ☐ b. Sylvia Saldívar said that the sweater belonged to Rachel.
   - ☐ c. Mrs. Price asked who the sweater belonged to.

3. Where is "Eleven" *set*?
   - ☐ a. in a school cafeteria
   - ☐ b. in a classroom
   - ☐ c. in a playground

4. The *mood* of the story is
   - ☐ a. comical.
   - ☐ b. mysterious.
   - ☐ c. sad.

LOOKING AT CLOZE. The following questions use the cloze technique to check your reading comprehension. Complete the paragraph by filling in each blank with one of the words listed below. Each word appears in the story. Since there are five words and four blanks, one of the words will not be used.

When seven or more people gather, the chances are surprisingly high that at least two will have been born on the same _____ and day. Obviously, the _____ people there are, the greater the odds. Ask the students in your _____ to write the month and day of their birth on a slip of paper. Later _____ will be amazed at how many people were born on the same date.

nonsense   class

month

everybody   more

NUMBER CORRECT	× 5 =	YOUR SCORE

NUMBER CORRECT	× 5 =	YOUR SCORE

LEARNING HOW TO READ CRITICALLY.
The following questions check your critical thinking skills. Put an *x* in the box next to each correct answer.

1. If Rachel had eventually left school with the sweater, it is likely that she would have
   ☐ a. shown it proudly to her parents.
   ☐ b. given it to someone as a present.
   ☐ c. thrown it away.

2. Clues in the story indicate that Rachel thought that Mrs. Price
   ☐ a. was one of her favorite teachers.
   ☐ b. didn't treat her fairly.
   ☐ c. would apologize to her later.

3. Although Rachel knew that later there would be a party with presents and that everyone would sing, "Happy birthday," she thought to herself, "Only it's too late." By this Rachel meant that
   ☐ a. she wasn't sure if her mother had time to make the cake she liked.
   ☐ b. she would probably get fewer presents than usual.
   ☐ c. the incident at school had ruined the day.

4. The vocabulary in "Eleven" is relatively easy. This is probably true because
   ☐ a. the narrator is eleven years old.
   ☐ b. the author has a limited vocabulary.
   ☐ c. there wasn't enough space in the story for more difficult words.

Improving Writing and Discussion Skills

- Rachel said that when you're eleven, "you're also ten, and nine, and eight, and seven, and six, and five, and four, and three, and two, and one" because "the way you grow old is kind of like . . . little wooden dolls that fit one inside the other, each year inside the next one." What did Rachel mean? Do you agree? Explain.
- After Rachel returned the sweater to Phyllis Lopez, Mrs. Price said nothing and pretended that everything was okay. *Was* everything okay? What might Mrs. Price have said or done?
- Rachel thought she wouldn't be happy at her birthday party. Do you believe that Rachel will feel any better by then—or will she still be unhappy?

Use the boxes below to total your scores for the exercises. Then write your score on pages 135 and 136.

☐ + **S**ELECTING DETAILS FROM THE STO[R]

☐ + **K**NOWING NEW VOCABULARY WORD[S]

☐ + **I**DENTIFYING STORY ELEMENTS

☐ + **L**OOKING AT CLOZE

☐ ▼ **L**EARNING HOW TO READ CRITICAL[LY]

☐ **S**core Total: Story 7

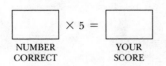

☐ × 5 = ☐

NUMBER CORRECT   YOUR SCORE

8. The Clearing

by Jesse Stuart

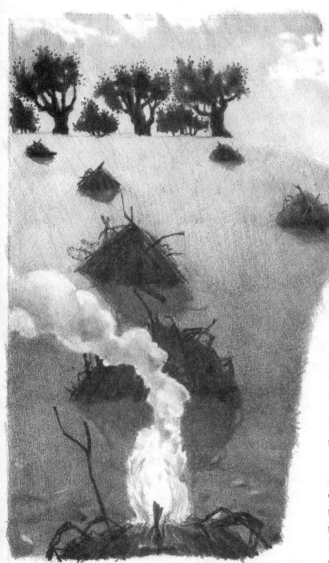

Meet the Author
Jesse Stuart (1907–1984) was born in
the Kentucky hill country, an area that is the
setting for many of his works. After gradu-
ating from Lincoln Memorial University, he
became an educator and writer. He has written
hundreds of short stories, numerous poems,
and many articles and books. Stuart's popular
autobiographical novel, *The Thread That Runs
So True*, is an account of his experiences
as a teacher in Kentucky and Ohio.

Finn and I were pruning the plum trees
around our garden when a rock came cracking
among the branches of the tree I was pruning.

"Where did that come from?" I asked
Finn, who was on the ground below piling
the branches.

"I don't know," he said.

Then we heard the Hinton boys laughing
on the other side of the valley. I went back
to pruning. In less than a minute, a rock hit
the limb above my head, and another rock
hit at Finn's feet. Then I came down from
the tree. Finn and I started throwing rocks.
In a few minutes, rocks were falling like
hailstones around them and around us. The
land was rocky on both sides of the valley,
and there were plenty of rocks to throw.

One of their rocks hit Finn on the foot,
and one of our rocks hit the largest Hinton
boy's head.

"Think of it," Finn said. "We fight before
we know each other's names! What will it
be as time goes on?"

We fought all afternoon with rocks. At

69

sunset the Hinton boys took off up the path and over the hill. We went home. When Pa asked why we hadn't finished pruning the trees, we told him.

"I told you," he said to Mom. "You'll see whether we can live apart!"

"Wait until we get to know each other," Mom said.

"But how are we ever going to know people like them?" Pa asked.

"Oh, something will happen," she replied calmly. "You'll see."

The next day, Mort Hinton was with his boys. They climbed higher on the hill, cutting the briers and brush and tree branches and stacking them neatly into piles. Finn and I pruned our trees.

"I'll say one thing for the Hintons," Mom said. "They're good workers."

"When they don't throw rocks," Finn said.

On the fourth day, my guinea hens[1] flew across the valley where the Hintons were clearing land.

"Get these hens back on your side of the valley," Mort Hinton yelled. "Get 'em back where they belong."

I didn't want to put my hens in the hen house. But I had to. I knew Mort Hinton would kill them. I wanted to tell him that they would help his land. They'd get rid of insects that might destroy his crop. But I was afraid to tell him anything.

A week had passed before my guinea hens got out and flew across the valley.

"If you don't keep your hens on your side of the valley," Mort Hinton hollered to me, "I'll wring their necks."

That night I put my guinea hens in again.

---
1. **guinea hens:** birds, similar to the pheasant, raised for their flavorful meat.

I fixed the hen house so they couldn't get out and roam the hills as they had always done. While Finn, Pa, and I cleared land on one side of the valley, the Hintons cleared on the other side.

Though we'd never been close enough to the Hintons to talk with them, and we didn't want to get that close, we found ourselves trying to do more work than the four of them. Each day, that early March, rain or sunshine, four Hintons worked on their side of the valley, and Pa, Finn, and I worked on our side. One day a Hinton boy hollered at us, "You can't clear as much land as we can."

"Don't answer him," Pa said.

When April came and the Hintons had finished clearing the hill and had burned the brush, Mort Hinton brought a skinny mule hitched to a plow and started plowing the new ground. He plowed slowly the first day. The second day my hens got out again and flew across the valley to the plowed ground. Mort Hinton caught two of them. The others flew back home when he tried to catch them. Then he yelled across to where we were plowing our new ground and told us what he had done.

"Your hens were on his land," Mom said. "He told you to keep them off his land."

Mort Hinton plowed his new ground by working from daylight until dusk, while the boys carried armloads of roots from the field and stacked them in great heaps. By the first of May, they had made this ground soil like a garden. Then came a rainy season in early May, and they carried baskets of tobacco plants and set them in the newly plowed rows.

"They're workers, all right," Pa said.

On a dark night about a week later, I watched a moving light from my upstairs window. It came from the direction of the Hintons', over the hill and down into the valley below our house. In a few minutes, I heard footsteps on the porch. Then there was a loud knock on our door. I heard Pa get out of bed and open the door.

"I'm Mort Hinton," a voice said. "My wife sent for your wife."

I heard Mom getting out of bed.

"I'll be ready in a minute," she called out.

Neither Pa nor Mort said another word.

"I'll be back when everything is all right," Mom said as she hurried off.

I watched the lantern fade from sight as Mort Hinton and Mom went down the path into the deep valley below the house. In two minutes or more, it flashed into sight again when they reached Hinton's tobacco field. The light moved swiftly up and over the hill.

The next morning, Pa cooked breakfast for us. He muttered about the Hintons as he stood near the hot stove frying eggs.

"They are friendly enough when they need something over there," Pa said.

We were ready to sit down to breakfast when Mom came home.

"Dollie Hinton's got a healthy girl baby," were Mom's first words as she sat down for a cup of coffee.

"What did they name the baby?" Glenna asked.

"They've not named her yet," Mom said. "I think they plan to call her Ethel. They're tickled to death. Three boys and now a girl!"

"What kind of people are they, anyway?" Pa asked.

"Like other people," Mom said. "They don't have much furniture in their house. They're working hard to pay for their farm."

"Will they be any better neighbors?" Pa asked.

"I think so," Mom said. "That hill over there is not a fence between us any longer."

"There's more than a hill between us," I said. "What about my hens Mort Hinton caught? Did he say anything about 'em last night?"

"And what about the Hinton boy that hit me on the foot with a rock?" Finn said. "I'd like to meet up with him sometime."

By the time we had finished our breakfast, Mort Hinton was plowing the young tobacco. His three sons were hoeing the tender plants with long-handled hoes.

"You'd think Mr. Hinton would be sleepy," Mom said. "He didn't go to bed last night. And the boys slept on the hay in the barn loft."

Pa, Finn, and I didn't have too much sympathy for the Hintons. Through the dining room window, we could look across the valley and watch Mort keep the plow moving steadily. We watched his boys dig with their hoes, never looking up from the ground.

"This will be a dry, sunny day," Pa said. "We'll burn the brush piles on the rest of our clearing."

We gathered our pitchforks, hoes, and rakes and went to the hill where we had cleared ground all spring. There were hundreds of brush piles on our twenty acres of cleared ground. The wind was still. The sun had dried the dew from the leaves that carpeted the ground between the brush piles.

"It's the right time to burn," Pa said. "I can't feel any wind. The brush has aged in these piles until it is as dry as powder."

Pa struck a match to the brush pile at the bottom of the clearing. The fire started with little leaps over the leaf-carpeted ground. Finn, Pa, and I set fire to the bottom of the clearing until we had a continuous line of fire going up the slope. Then a wind sprang up from nowhere. And when flames leaped from brush pile to brush pile, Pa looked at me.

"This is out of control," Pa said. "Grab a hoe and start raking a ring."

"I'm afraid we can't stop it," Finn said. "We'll have to work fast to save the orchards."

"Run to the house and get Sal and Glenna," Pa yelled.

"Look, Pa," Finn said, pointing down the hill.

Mort Hinton was in front. He was running up the hill. His three sons were running behind him, each with a hoe across his shoulder.

"It's out of control," Pa shouted to Mort before he reached us.

"We've come to help," Mort said.

"Can we keep it from the orchards?" Pa asked.

"Let's run to the top of the hill and fire against it," Mort said. "I've burned hundreds of acres of clearings on hillsides, and I always fire the top first and let it burn down! I fire the bottom last. Maybe we'll not be too late to save the orchards!"

Mort ran up the hill and we followed. Finn and I didn't speak to his boys and they didn't speak to us. But when we started raking a ring side by side, we started talking to the Hintons. We forgot about the rock fight. Now wasn't the time to remember it, when flames down under the hill were shooting twenty to thirty feet high. In no time, we raked the ring across the top of the clearing. And the fire Mort Hinton set along the ring burned fiercely down the hill and made the ring wider and wider. Only once did fire blow across the ring, and Pa stopped it then.

As soon as we had this spot under control, we raked a ring down the west side near the peach orchard. Mort set a line of fire along this ring and let it burn toward the middle of the clearing. Then we raked a ring on the east side and fired against the fire that was approaching our plum trees and our house. Soon the leaping flames met in the clearing. We had the fire under control. Our clearing was burned clean as a whistle.

"How much do I owe you?" Pa asked Mort Hinton.

"You don't owe me anything," Mort said. "We're just paying you back for the help your wife gave us."

"Then let's go to the house for dinner," Pa said.

"Some other time," Mort said. "We must go home and see about Dollie and the baby."

As we went down the hill, Finn and I talked with the Hinton boys about fishing and wild-bee trees, while Pa and Mort laughed and talked about weather and crops.

SELECTING DETAILS FROM THE STORY.
The following questions help you check your reading comprehension. Put an *x* in the box next to each correct answer.

1. The first sign of trouble between the two families was
   - ☐ a. a dispute over a piece of land.
   - ☐ b. an argument regarding some hens.
   - ☐ c. a rock fight across the valley.

2. Pa and the others agreed that the Hintons were
   - ☐ a. good workers.
   - ☐ b. very lazy.
   - ☐ c. quite selfish.

3. When the fire raged out of control, the Hintons
   - ☐ a. ignored their neighbors' problems and went about their work.
   - ☐ b. rushed up the hill to help.
   - ☐ c. didn't know how to contain the fire.

4. When Pa offered to pay Mort Hinton, Mr. Hinton said that
   - ☐ a. he would send him a bill.
   - ☐ b. he would accept a dinner as payment for the work.
   - ☐ c. Pa didn't owe him anything.

KNOWING NEW VOCABULARY WORDS.
The following questions check your vocabulary skills. Put an *x* in the box next to each correct answer.

1. The boys were pruning the plum tree, when a rock came crashing through the branches. Which of the following best defines the word *pruning*?
   - ☐ a. packing
   - ☐ b. constructing
   - ☐ c. cutting

2. "If you don't keep your hens on your side of the valley, I'll wring their necks," Mort Hinton hollered. What is the meaning of the word *wring*?
   - ☐ a. twist
   - ☐ b. clean
   - ☐ c. cover

3. They climbed up the hill, "cutting the briers and brush and tree branches," and stacking them neatly into piles. What are *briers*?
   - ☐ a. food
   - ☐ b. bushes
   - ☐ c. earth

4. Mr. Hinton had been up all night yet was out plowing his field very early the next morning. The neighbors didn't have much sympathy for him. When you have *sympathy*, you
   - ☐ a. mind your own business.
   - ☐ b. care about another person's trouble.
   - ☐ c. believe that people deserve whatever they get.

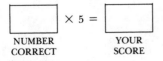

NUMBER CORRECT   × 5 =   YOUR SCORE

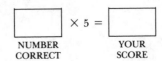

NUMBER CORRECT   × 5 =   YOUR SCORE

IDENTIFYING STORY ELEMENTS. The following questions check your knowledge of story elements. Put an *x* in the box next to each correct answer.

1. In "The Clearing," there is *conflict* between
   - ☐ a. Pa and Finn.
   - ☐ b. Finn and his brothers.
   - ☐ c. Pa's sons and the Hinton boys.

2. The *climax*, or turning point of the story, occurred when
   - ☐ a. the hens flew onto the Hinton's land.
   - ☐ b. the fire leaped out of control.
   - ☐ c. Mrs. Hinton had a baby girl.

3. Which of the following *foreshadows* the ending of the story?
   - ☐ a. When Pa asked how they would even get to know the Hintons, Mom said, "Oh, something will happen."
   - ☐ b. When a Hinton boy hollered across the valley, Pa said, "Don't answer him."
   - ☐ c. When Mom said that the Hintons were "working hard to pay for their farm."

4. Identify the statement that best expresses the *theme* of the story.
   - ☐ a. By helping each other during a crisis, two quarreling families become friendly neighbors.
   - ☐ b. Working on a farm is very dangerous.
   - ☐ c. Often neighbors feud with each other for foolish reasons.

☐ × 5 = ☐

NUMBER
CORRECT

YOUR
SCORE

LOOKING AT CLOZE. The following questions use the cloze technique to check your reading comprehension. Complete the paragraph by filling in each blank with one of the words listed below. Each word appears in the story. Since there are five words and four blanks, one of the words will not be used.

On October 8, 1871, a huge fire swept through the city of Chicago, _____ the entire business district. The fire burned out of _____ for more than a day, leaving approximately 100,000 people homeless. Legend has it that the fire started when a cow owned by a Mrs. Patrick O'Leary knocked over a lighted _____ . According to the tale, a barn caught fire, and gusting winds quickly spread the _____ .

lantern   flames

destroying

control   continuous

☐ × 5 = ☐

NUMBER
CORRECT

YOUR
SCORE

LEARNING HOW TO READ CRITICALLY.
The following questions check your critical thinking skills. Put an *x* in the box next to each correct answer.

1. The "Clearing" in the title of the story refers not only to the land but also to the
   □ a. "clearing of the air," or of the bad feelings, between the families.
   □ b. idea that nobody in the story is free from, or clear of, blame.
   □ c. facts that the two families stayed clear of each other.

2. Which statement is true?
   □ a. Mort Hinton never helped put out a fire before.
   □ b. Guinea hens often destroy crops.
   □ c. Mom assisted Mrs. Hinton when she gave birth.

3. When Mom said, "That hill over there is not a fence between us any longer," she was suggesting that the
   □ a. relationship between the two families would grow even worse.
   □ b. barriers between the two families were coming down.
   □ c. Hintons had plowed most of the land on the hill.

4. The last paragraph of the story indicates that the two families
   □ a. had many things in common.
   □ b. still felt uncomfortable with each other.
   □ c. will soon be feuding again.

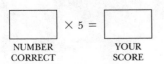

NUMBER CORRECT   × 5 =   YOUR SCORE

Improving Writing and Discussion Skills

- From the beginning of the story Mom is more accepting of the Hintons than are the other members of her family. Do you agree or disagree with this statement? Offer evidence to support your answer.
- Finn said, "We fight before we know each other's names! What will it be as time goes on?" What is the meaning of these words? Do you think it likely that the two families will ever have dinner together? Why?
- Identify two *different* kinds of encounters in the story. Briefly describe each.

Use the boxes below to total your scores for the exercises. Then write your score on pages 135 and 136.

[ ] **SELECTING DETAILS FROM THE STORY**
+
[ ] **KNOWING NEW VOCABULARY WORDS**
+
[ ] **IDENTIFYING STORY ELEMENTS**
+
[ ] **LOOKING AT CLOZE**
+
[ ] **LEARNING HOW TO READ CRITICALLY**
▼
[ ] **Score Total:** Story 8

9. The Medicine Bag

by Virginia Driving Hawk Sneve

My kid sister Cheryl and I always bragged about our Sioux grandpa, Joe Iron Shell. Our friends, who had always lived in the city and only knew about Indians from movies and TV, were impressed by our stories. Maybe we exaggerated and made Grandpa and the reservation sound glamorous; but when we'd return home to Iowa after our yearly summer visit to Grandpa, we always had some exciting tale to tell.

We always had some authentic Sioux article to show our listeners. One year Cheryl had new moccasins that Grandpa had made. On another visit he gave me a small, round, flat, rawhide drum which was decorated with a painting of a warrior riding a horse. He taught me a real Sioux chant to sing while I beat the drum with a leather-covered stick that had a feather on the end. Man, that really made an impression.

We never showed our friends Grandpa's picture. Not that we were ashamed of him, but because we knew that the glamorous tales we told didn't go with the real thing. Our

Meet the Author

Virginia Driving Hawk Sneve (1933–   ) was born and grew up on the Rosebud Sioux Reservation in South Dakota. As "The Medicine Bag" suggests, Sneve often draws on personal experiences for the subject matter of her work. In addition to her stories, Sneve has written many children's books, four novels, and a number of articles and poems. Among her books about native American life are *The Sioux, Jimmy Yellow Hawk,* and *High Elk's Treasure.* She is also the editor of *Dancing Teepees: Poems of Native American Youth.*

friends would have laughed at the picture, because Grandpa wasn't tall and stately like TV Indians. His hair wasn't in braids, but hung in stringy, gray strands on his neck; and he was old. He was our great-grandfather, and he didn't live in a tipi, but all by himself in a part log, part tar-paper shack on the Rosebud Reservation in South Dakota. So when Grandpa came to visit us, I was so ashamed and embarrassed, I could've died.

There are a lot of yippy poodles and other fancy little dogs in our neighborhood; but they usually barked singly at the mailman from the safety of their own yards. Now it sounded as if a whole pack of mutts were barking together in one place.

I got up and walked to the curb to see what the commotion was. About a block away I saw a crowd of little kids yelling, with the dogs yipping and growling around someone who was walking down the middle of the street.

I watched the group as it slowly came closer, and saw that in the center of the strange procession was a man wearing a tall black hat. He'd pause now and then to peer at something in his hand and then at the houses on either side of the street. I felt cold and hot at the same time as I recognized the man. "Oh, no!" I whispered. "It's Grandpa!"

I stood on the curb, unable to move even though I wanted to run and hide. Then I got mad when I saw how the yippy dogs were growling and nipping at the old man's baggy pant legs, and how wearily he poked them away with his cane. "Stupid mutts," I said as I ran to rescue Grandpa.

When I kicked and hollered at the dogs to get away, they put their tails between their legs and scattered. The kids ran to the curb where they watched me and the old man.

"Grandpa," I said and felt pretty dumb when my voice cracked. I reached for his beat-up old tin suitcase, which was tied shut with a rope. But he set it down right in the street and shook my hand.

"*Hau, Takoza,* Grandchild," he greeted me formally in Sioux.

All I could do was stand there with the whole neighborhood watching and shake the hand of the leather-brown old man. I saw how his gray hair straggled from under his big black hat, which had a drooping feather in its crown. His rumpled black suit hung like a sack over his stooped frame. As he shook my hand, his coat fell open to expose a bright-red, satin shirt with a beaded bolo tie under the collar. His getup wasn't out of place on the reservation; but it sure was here, and I wanted to sink right through the pavement.

"Hi," I muttered with my head down. I tried to pull my hand away when I felt his bony hand trembling, and looked up to see fatigue in his face. I felt like crying. I couldn't think of anything to say, so I picked up Grandpa's suitcase, took his arm, and guided him up the driveway to our house.

Mom was standing on the steps. I don't know how long she'd been watching, but her hand was over her mouth and she looked as if she couldn't believe what she saw. Then she ran to us.

"Grandpa," she gasped. "How in the world did you get here?"

She checked her move to embrace Grandpa and I remembered that such a display of affection is unseemly to the Sioux and would embarrass him.

"*Hau,* Marie," he said as he shook Mom's hand. She smiled and took his other arm.

As we supported him up the steps, the door

banged open and Cheryl came bursting out of the house. She was all smiles, and was so obviously glad to see Grandpa that I was ashamed of how I felt.

"Grandpa!" she yelled happily. "You came to see us!"

Grandpa smiled and Mom and I let go of him as he stretched out his arms to my ten-year-old sister, who was still young enough to be hugged.

"*Wicincala,* little girl," he greeted her and then collapsed.

He had fainted. Mom and I carried him into her sewing room, where we had a spare bed.

After we had Grandpa on the bed, Mom stood there helplessly patting his shoulder.

"Shouldn't we call the doctor, Mom?" I suggested, since she didn't seem to know what to do.

"Yes," she agreed with a sigh. "You make Grandpa comfortable, Martin."

I reluctantly moved to the bed. I knew Grandpa wouldn't want to have Mom undress him, but I didn't want to, either. He was so skinny and frail that his coat slipped off easily. When I loosened his tie and opened his shirt collar, I felt a small leather pouch that hung from a thong around his neck. I left it alone and moved to remove his boots. The scuffed old cowboy boots were tight, and he moaned as I put pressure on his legs to jerk them off.

I put the boots on the floor and saw why they fit so tight. Each one was stuffed with money. I looked at the bills that lined the boots and started to ask about them; but Grandpa's eyes were closed again.

Mom came back with a basin of water. "The doctor thinks Grandpa is suffering from heat exhaustion," she explained as she bathed Grandpa's face. Mom gave a big sigh, "*Oh hinh,* Martin. How do you suppose he got here?"

We found out after the doctor's visit. Grandpa was angrily sitting up in bed while Mom tried to feed him some soup.

"Tonight you let Marie feed you, Grandpa," spoke my dad, who had gotten home from work just as the doctor was leaving. "You're not really sick," he said as he gently pushed Grandpa back against the pillows. "The doctor said you just got too tired and hot after your long trip."

Grandpa relaxed, and between sips of soup he told of his journey. Soon after our visit to him, Grandpa decided that he would like to see where his only living descendants lived and what our home was like. Besides, he admitted sheepishly, he was lonesome after we left.

I knew everybody felt as guilty as I did—especially Mom. Mom was all Grandpa had left. So even after she married my dad, who's a white man and teaches in the college in our city, and after Cheryl and I were born, Mom made sure that every summer we spent a week with Grandpa.

I never thought that Grandpa would be lonely after our visits, and none of us noticed how old and weak he had become. But Grandpa knew, and so he came to us. He had ridden on buses for two and a half days. When he arrived in the city, tired and stiff from sitting for so long, he set out, walking, to find us.

He had stopped to rest on the steps of some building downtown, and a policeman found him. The cop, according to Grandpa, was a good man who took him to the bus stop and waited until the bus came, and told the driver to let Grandpa out at Bell View Drive. After Grandpa got off the bus, he started walking again. But he couldn't see the house numbers on the other side when he walked on the sidewalk, so he walked in the middle of the street. That's when all the little kids and the dogs followed him.

I knew everybody felt as bad as I did. Yet I was proud of this eighty-six-year-old man, who had never been away from the reservation, having the courage to travel so far alone.

"You found the money in my boots?" he asked Mom.

"Martin did," she answered, and roused herself to scold. "Grandpa, you shouldn't have carried so much money. What if someone had stolen it from you?"

Grandpa laughed. "I would've known if anyone tried to take the boots off my feet. The money is what I've saved for a long time—a hundred dollars—for my funeral. But you take it now to buy groceries so that I won't be a burden to you while I am here."

"That won't be necessary, Grandpa," Dad said. "We are honored to have you with us, and you will never be a burden. I am only sorry that we never thought to bring you home with us this summer and spare you the discomfort of a long trip."

Grandpa was pleased. "Thank you," he answered. "But do not feel bad that you didn't bring me with you, for I would not have come then. It was not time." He said this in such a way that no one could argue with him. To Grandpa and the Sioux, he once told me, a thing would be done when it was the right time to do it, and that's the way it was.

"Also," Grandpa went on, looking at me, "I have come because it is soon time for Martin to have the medicine bag."

We all knew what that meant. Grandpa thought he was going to die, and he had to follow the tradition of his family to pass the medicine bag, along with its history, to the oldest male child.

"Even though the boy," he said still looking at me, "bears a white man's name, the medicine bag will be his."

I didn't know what to say. I had the same hot and cold feeling that I had when I first saw Grandpa in the street. The medicine bag was the dirty leather pouch I had found around his neck. "I could never wear such a thing," I almost said aloud. I thought of having my friends see it in gym class, at the swimming pool, and could imagine the smart things they would say. But I just swallowed hard and took a step toward the bed. I knew I would have to take it.

But Grandpa was tired. "Not now, Martin," he said, waving his hand in dismissal, "it is not time. Now I will sleep."

So that's how Grandpa came to be with us for two months. My friends kept asking to come see the old man, but I put them off. I told myself that I didn't want them laughing at Grandpa. But even as I made excuses, I knew it wasn't Grandpa that I was afraid they'd laugh at.

Nothing bothered Cheryl about bringing her friends to see Grandpa. Every day after school started, there'd be a crew of giggling little girls or round-eyed little boys crowded around the old man on the patio, where he'd gotten in the habit of sitting every afternoon.

Grandpa would smile in his gentle way and patiently answer their questions, or he'd tell them stories of brave warriors, ghosts, animals; and the kids listened in awed silence. Those little guys thought Grandpa was great.

Finally, one day after school, my friends came home with me because nothing I said stopped them. "We're going to see the great

Indian of Bell View Drive," said Hank, who was supposed to be my best friend. "My brother has seen him three times, so he oughta be well enough to see us."

When we got to my house, Grandpa was sitting on the patio. He had on his red shirt; but today he also wore a fringed leather vest that was decorated with beads. Instead of his usual cowboy boots, he had solidly beaded moccasins on his feet that stuck out of his black trousers. Of course, he had his old black hat on—he was seldom without it. But it had been brushed and the feather in the beaded headband was proudly erect, its tip a brighter white. His hair lay in silver strands over the red shirt collar.

I stared just as my friends did, and I heard one of them murmur, "Wow!"

Grandpa looked up, and when his eyes met mine, they twinkled as if he was laughing inside. He nodded to me and my face got all hot. I could tell that he had known all along I was afraid he'd embarrass me in front of my friends.

"*Hau, hoksilas,* boys," he greeted and held out his hand.

My buddies passed in a single file and shook his hand as I introduced them. They were so polite, I almost laughed. "How, there, Grandpa," and even a "How-do-you-do, sir."

"You look fine, Grandpa," I said as the boys sat on the lawn chairs or on the patio floor.

"*Hanh,* yes," he agreed. "When I woke up this morning it seemed the right time to dress in the good clothes. I knew that my grandson would be bringing his friends."

"You guys want some lemonade or something?" I offered. No one answered. They were listening to Grandpa as he started telling how he'd killed the deer from which his vest was made.

Grandpa did most of the talking while my friends were there. I was so proud of him, and amazed at how respectfully quiet my buddies were. Mom had to chase them home at supper time. As they left they shook Grandpa's hand again and said to me:

"Martin, he's really great!"

"Yeah, man! Don't blame you for keeping him to yourself."

"Can we come back?"

But after they left, Mom said, "No more visitors for a while, Martin. Grandpa won't admit it, but his strength hasn't returned. He likes having company, but it tires him."

That evening, Grandpa called me to his room before he went to sleep. "Tomorrow," he said, "when you come home, it will be time to give you the medicine bag."

I felt a hard squeeze from where my heart is supposed to be and was scared, but I answered, "OK, Grandpa."

All night I had weird dreams about thunder and lightning on a high hill. From a distance I heard the slow beat of a drum. When I woke up in the morning, I felt as if I hadn't sleep at all. At school it seemed as if the day would never end and, when it finally did, I ran home.

Grandpa was in his room, sitting on the bed. The shades were down and the place was dim and cool. I sat on the floor in front of Grandpa; but he didn't even look at me. After what seemed a long time he spoke.

"I sent your mother and sister away. What you will hear today is only for a man's ears. What you will receive is only for a man's hands." He fell silent and I felt shivers down my back.

"My father in his early manhood," Grandpa began, "made a vision quest to find a spirit guide for his life. You cannot understand how it was in that time, when the great Teton Sioux were first made to stay on the reservation. There was a strong need for guidance from *Wakantanka,* the Great Spirit. But too many of the young men were filled with despair and hatred. They thought it was hopeless to search for a vision when the glorious life was gone, and only the hated confines of a reservation lay ahead. But my father held to the old ways.

"He carefully prepared for his quest with a purifying sweat bath and then he went alone to a high butte top to fast and pray. After three days, he received his sacred dream—in which he found, after long searching, the white man's iron. He did not understand his vision of finding something belonging to the white people; for in that time, they were the enemy. When he came down from the butte to cleanse himself at the stream below, he found the remains of a campfire and the broken shell of an iron kettle. This was a sign which reinforced his dream. He took a piece of the iron for his medicine bag, which he had made of elk skin years before, to prepare for his quest.

"He returned to his village, where he told his dream to the wise old men of the tribe. They gave him the name *Iron Shell;* but neither did they understand the meaning of the dream. This first Iron Shell kept the piece of iron with him at all times and believed it gave him protection from the evils of those unhappy days.

"Then a terrible thing happened to Iron Shell. He and several other young men were taken from their homes by the soldiers, and sent far away to a white man's boarding school. He was angry and lonesome for his parents and the young girl he had wed before he was taken away. At first Iron Shell resisted the teachers' attempts to change him, and he did not try to learn. One day it was his turn to work in the school's blacksmith shop. As he walked into the place, he knew that his medicine had brought him there to learn and work with the white man's iron.

"Iron Shell became a blacksmith and worked at the trade when he returned to the reservation. All of his life he treasured the medicine bag. When he was old, and I was a man, he gave it to me; for no one made the vision quest any more."

Grandpa quit talking and I stared in disbelief as he covered his face with his hands. His shoulders were shaking with quiet sobs, and I looked away until he began to speak again.

"I kept the bag until my son, your mother's father, was a man and had to leave us to fight in the war across the ocean. I gave him the bag, for I believed it would protect him in battle; but he did not take it with him. He was afraid that he would lose it. He died in a faraway place."

Again Grandpa was still and I felt his grief around me.

"My son," he went on after clearing his throat, "had only a daughter and it is not proper for her to know of these things."

He unbuttoned his shirt, pulled out the leather pouch, and lifted it over his head. He held it in his hand, turning it over and over as if memorizing how it looked.

"In the bag," he said as he opened it and removed two objects, "is the broken shell of the iron kettle, a pebble from the butte, and a piece of the sacred sage."[1] He held the pouch upside down and dust drifted down.

---

1. **sage:** a plant thought by some to have healing powers. Its leaves are sometimes used in medicine.

"After the bag is yours, you must put a piece of prairie sage within and never open it again until you pass it on to your son." He replaced the pebble and the piece of iron, and tied the bag.

I stood up, somehow knowing I should. Grandpa slowly rose from the bed and stood upright in front of me holding the bag before my face. I closed my eyes and waited for him to slip it over my head. But he spoke.

"No, you need not wear it." He placed the soft leather bag in my right hand and closed my other hand over it. "It would not be right to wear it in this time and place where no one will understand. Put it safely away until you are again on the reservation. Wear it then, when you replace the sacred sage."

Grandpa turned and sat again on the bed. Wearily he leaned his head against the pillow. "Go," he said, "I will sleep now."

"Thank you, Grandpa," I said softly, and left with the bag in my hands.

That night Mom and Dad took Grandpa to the hospital. Two weeks later, I stood alone on the lonely prairie of the reservation and put the sacred sage in my medicine bag.

SELECTING DETAILS FROM THE STORY.
The following questions help you check your
reading comprehension. Put an *x* in the box
next to each correct answer.

1. When Martin's friends visited Grandpa,
   they were
   - ☐ a. bored by his tales.
   - ☐ b. fascinated by his stories.
   - ☐ c. not very polite.

2. Grandpa's boots fit very tightly because
   - ☐ a. they were much too small for him.
   - ☐ b. they were stuffed with money.
   - ☐ c. his feet swelled as a result of the long
     journey.

3. The purpose of Grandpa's visit was to
   - ☐ a. pass the medicine bag and its history
     to Martin.
   - ☐ b. take a well-earned vacation.
   - ☐ c. visit a different part of the country.

4. The medicine bag contained
   - ☐ a. items usually found in a first-aid kit.
   - ☐ b. a number of very valuable coins.
   - ☐ c. a pebble, a piece of iron, and sacred
     sage.

KNOWING NEW VOCABULARY WORDS. The
following questions check your vocabulary
skills. Put an *x* in the box next to each correct
answer.

1. They showed their friends authentic Sioux
   articles, such as moccasins Grandpa had
   made and a drum decorated with a
   painting of a warrior. The word *authentic*
   means
   - ☐ a. broken or damaged.
   - ☐ b. genuine or real.
   - ☐ c. enormous or huge.

2. The old man's rumpled black suit hung
   like a sack over his frame. The word
   rumpled means
   - ☐ a. wrinkled.
   - ☐ b. stylish.
   - ☐ c. narrow.

3. A small pouch hung from a thong around
   his neck. A *thong* is a
   - ☐ a. bracelet.
   - ☐ b. narrow strip of leather.
   - ☐ c. deep cut.

4. Grandpa had ridden on buses for two and
   a half days, and he arrived tired and weak
   from the discomfort of the trip. Which
   expression best defines the word *discomfort*?
   - ☐ a. pain or distress
   - ☐ b. enjoyment or pleasure
   - ☐ c. cost or fee

☐ × 5 = ☐

NUMBER
CORRECT

YOUR
SCORE

☐ × 5 = ☐

NUMBER
CORRECT

YOUR
SCORE

IDENTIFYING STORY ELEMENTS. The following questions check your knowledge of story elements. Put an *x* in the box next to each correct answer.

1. Who is the *narrator* in "The Medicine Bag"?
   - ☐ a. Martin
   - ☐ b. Grandpa
   - ☐ c. Cheryl

2. What happened first in the *plot* of the story?
   - ☐ a. Grandpa placed the medicine bag in Martin's hand.
   - ☐ b. The doctor said that Grandpa was probably suffering from heat exhaustion.
   - ☐ c. Grandpa told Martin the story of Iron Shell.

3. What was Martin's *motive* for going to the reservation?
   - ☐ a. to tell Grandpa's friends there about Grandpa
   - ☐ b. to claim Grandpa's possessions
   - ☐ c. to find some sacred sage for the medicine bag

4. The *mood* of "The Medicine Bag" is
   - ☐ a. shocking.
   - ☐ b. serious.
   - ☐ c. humorous.

LOOKING AT CLOZE. The following questions use the cloze technique to check your reading comprehension. Complete the paragraph by filling in each blank with one of the words listed below. Each word appears in the story. Since there are five words and four blanks, one of the words will not be used.

Because of its sunny climate, South

_____ has been nicknamed
            1

the Sunshine State. But did you know that

the state of South Dakota takes its *real*

_____ from a Sioux Indian
            2

word? The _____ called
                 3

themselves *Dakota,* which means "allies"

or "friends." The word *Dakota* also

_____ "the land of the free."
            4

Sioux   collapsed

Dakota

name   meant

NUMBER CORRECT ☐ × 5 = ☐ YOUR SCORE

NUMBER CORRECT ☐ × 5 = ☐ YOUR SCORE

LEARNING HOW TO READ CRITICALLY.
The following questions check your critical
thinking skills. Put an *x* in the box next to
each correct answer.

1. The last paragraph of the story leads us
   to conclude that Grandpa
   ☐ a. took the bus back to South Dakota.
   ☐ b. recovered later at his daughter's
         house.
   ☐ c. died after arriving at the hospital.

2. Iron Shell was probably given that name
   ☐ a. because he was so strong.
   ☐ b. because he later became a
         blacksmith.
   ☐ c. as a result of the dream he had.

3. Story clues suggest that Grandpa came
   to visit because he
   ☐ a. suddenly grew lonely for his family.
   ☐ b. knew he was going to die soon.
   ☐ c. wanted to give his family some
         money.

4. According to tradition, Martin must
   eventually pass the medicine bag to
   ☐ a. the oldest male child in his family.
   ☐ b. his youngest child.
   ☐ c. one of his parents.

Improving Writing and Discussion Skills

● Although Martin always bragged
   about his grandfather, when Grandpa
   arrived Martin was ashamed and
   embarrassed. Why? Did Martin's fears
   prove to be founded? Explain.
● Why was Martin distressed at the
   thought of wearing the medicine bag?
   Do you think Grandpa realized this?
   Give reasons for your answer.
● According to Grandpa, "A thing
   would be done when it was the right
   time to do it." What does this mean
   and how does it apply to Martin and
   Grandpa?

Use the boxes below to total your scores
for the exercises. Then write your score on
pages 135 and 136.

☐   **S**ELECTING DETAILS FROM THE STO[RY]
 +
☐   **K**NOWING NEW VOCABULARY WORD[S]
 +
☐   **I**DENTIFYING STORY ELEMENTS
 +
☐   **L**OOKING AT CLOZE
 +
☐   **L**EARNING HOW TO READ CRITICAL[LY]
 ▼
☐   **S**core Total: Story 9

☐ × 5 = ☐

NUMBER   YOUR
CORRECT   SCORE

86

10. The Fun They Had
by Isaac Asimov

Meet the Author

Isaac Asimov (1920–1992) has written so many novels and short stories that he once confessed even he had lost count. Certainly his books, on a wide variety of subjects, number well over four hundred. Born in Russia, Asimov moved to the United States at the age of three. After earning a Ph.D. at Columbia University, he taught at various colleges. Asimov's novels include *I Robot* and *The Robots of Dawn*. *Best Science Fiction of Isaac Asimov* is one of his most popular story collections.

*M*argie even wrote about it that night in her diary. On the page headed May 17, 2157, she wrote, "Today Tommy found a real book!"

It was a very old book. Margie's grandfather once said that when he was a little boy *his* grandfather told him that there was a time when all stories were printed on paper.

They turned the pages, which were yellow and crinkly, and it was awfully funny to read words that stood still instead of moving the way they were supposed to—on a screen, you know. And then, when they turned back to the page before, it had the same words on it that it had had when they read it the first time.

"Gee," said Tommy, "what a waste. When you're through with the book, you just throw it away, I guess. Our television screen must have had a million books on it and it's good for plenty more. I wouldn't throw *it* away."

"Same with mine," said Margie. She was eleven and hadn't seen as many telebooks as Tommy had. He was thirteen.

She said, "Where did you find it?"

"In my house." He pointed without looking, because he was busy reading. "In the attic."

"What's it about?"

"School."

Margie was scornful. "School? What's there to write about school? I hate school."

Margie always hated school, but now she hated it more than ever. The mechanical teacher had been giving her test after test in geography and she had been doing worse and worse until her mother had shaken her head sorrowfully and sent for the County Inspector.

He was a round little man with a red face and a whole box of tools with dials and wires. He smiled at Margie and gave her an apple, then took the teacher apart. Margie had hoped he wouldn't know how to put it together again, but he knew how all right, and, after an hour or so, there it was again, large and square and ugly, with a big screen on which all the lessons were shown and the questions were asked. That wasn't so bad. The part Margie hated most was the slot where she had to put homework and test papers. She always had to write them out in a punch code they made her learn when she was six years old, and the mechanical teacher calculated the mark in no time.

The Inspector had smiled after he was finished and patted Margie's head. He said to her mother, "It's not the little girl's fault, Mrs. Jones. I think the geography sector was geared a little too quick. Those things happen sometimes. I've slowed it up to an average ten-year level. Actually, the over-all pattern of her progress is quite satisfactory."

And he patted Margie's head again.

Margie was disappointed. She had been hoping they would take the teacher away altogether. They had once taken Tommy's teacher away for nearly a month because the history sector had blanked out completely.

So she said to Tommy, "Why would anyone write about school?"

Tommy looked at her with very superior eyes. "Because it's not our kind of school, stupid. This is the old kind of school that they had hundreds and hundreds of years ago." He added loftily, pronouncing the word carefully, "*Centuries* ago."

Margie was hurt. "Well, I don't know what kind of school they had all that time ago." She read the book over his shoulder for a while, then said, "Anyway, they had a teacher."

"Sure they had a teacher, but it wasn't a *regular* teacher. It was a man."

"A man? How could a man be a teacher?"

"Well, he just told the boys and girls things and gave them homework and asked them questions."

"A man isn't smart enough."

"Sure he is. My father knows as much as my teacher."

"He can't. A man can't know as much as a teacher."

"He knows almost as much, I betcha."

Margie wasn't prepared to dispute that. She said, "I wouldn't want a strange man in my house to teach me."

Tommy screamed with laughter. "You don't know much, Margie. The teachers didn't live in the house. They had a special building and all the kids went there."

"And all the kids learned the same thing?"

"Sure, if they were the same age."

"But my mother says a teacher has to be adjusted to fit the mind of each boy and girl it teaches and that each kid has to be taught differently."

"Just the same they didn't do it that way then. If you don't like it, you don't have to read the book."

"I didn't say I didn't like it," Margie said quickly. She wanted to read about those funny schools.

They weren't even half-finished when Margie's mother called, "Margie! School!"

Margie looked up. "Not yet, Mamma."

"Now!" said Mrs. Jones. "And it's probably time for Tommy, too."

Margie said to Tommy, "Can I read the book some more with you after school?"

"Maybe," he said nonchalantly. He walked away whistling, the dusty old book tucked beneath his arm.

Margie went into the schoolroom. It was right next to her bedroom, and the mechanical teacher was on and waiting for her. It was always on at the same time every day except Saturday and Sunday, because her mother said little girls learned better if they learned at regular hours.

The screen was lit up, and it said: "Today's arithmetic lesson is on the addition of proper fractions. Please insert yesterday's homework in the proper slot."

Margie did so with a sigh. She was thinking about the old schools they had when her grandfather's grandfather was a little boy. All the kids from the whole neighborhood came, laughing and shouting in the schoolyard, sitting together in the schoolroom, going home together at the end of the day. They learned the same things, so they could help one another on the homework and talk about it.

And the teachers were people. . . .

The mechanical teacher was flashing on the screen: "When we add the fractions 1/2 and 1/4 ——"

Margie was thinking about how the kids must have loved it in the old days. She was thinking about the fun they had.

SELECTING DETAILS FROM THE STORY.
The following questions help you check your reading comprehension. Put an *x* in the box next to each correct answer.

1. Margie and Tommy were surprised that the words in the old book
   - ☐ a. had changed so much in meaning.
   - ☐ b. were spelled so strangely.
   - ☐ c. stood still instead of moving on a screen.

2. The County Inspector told Mrs. Jones that
   - ☐ a. Margie was making slow progress in school.
   - ☐ b. they would send a new teacher to the house.
   - ☐ c. the mechanical teacher needed an adjustment.

3. According to Tommy, the schools of long ago
   - ☐ a. were very similar to the present day schools.
   - ☐ b. were special buildings where boys and girls went to be taught.
   - ☐ c. had a different teacher for each student who attended.

4. What Margie liked about the old schools was that
   - ☐ a. everyone who went to them always got high marks.
   - ☐ b. the students did things together, and the teachers were people.
   - ☐ c. there were no classes on Saturday and Sunday.

☐ × 5 = ☐

NUMBER CORRECT   YOUR SCORE

KNOWING NEW VOCABULARY WORDS. The following questions check your vocabulary skills. Put an *x* in the box next to each correct answer.

1. Tommy found a very old book whose pages were yellow and crinkly. The word *crinkly* means
   - ☐ a. wrinkled.
   - ☐ b. shiny.
   - ☐ c. smooth.

2. In no time at all, the mechanical teacher calculated what mark to give Margie's test papers. Which of the following best defines the word *calculated*?
   - ☐ a. erased
   - ☐ b. figured out
   - ☐ c. improved

3. Margie had been doing poorly in the geography sector because the tests were a little too difficult. As used here, the word *sector* means
   - ☐ a. section or part.
   - ☐ b. arithmetic or math.
   - ☐ c. learning or studying.

4. When Margie asked if she could read the book, Tommy answered, "Maybe," nonchalantly, as he walked away whistling. When you act *nonchalantly*, you are
   - ☐ a. frightened.
   - ☐ b. ill at ease.
   - ☐ c. unconcerned.

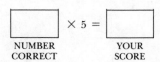

NUMBER CORRECT   YOUR SCORE

IDENTIFYING STORY ELEMENTS. The following questions check your knowledge of story elements. Put an *x* in the box next to each correct answer.

1. "The Fun They Had" is *set* in a
   - ☐ a. school many years ago.
   - ☐ b. TV repair shop at the present time.
   - ☐ c. home in the future.

2. Who is the *main character* in the story?
   - ☐ a. Tommy
   - ☐ b. Margie
   - ☐ c. the County Inspector

3. What happened last in the *plot* of "The Fun They Had"?
   - ☐ a. Margie looked at the lesson on fractions on the screen.
   - ☐ b. The County Inspector took the mechanical teacher apart.
   - ☐ c. Tommy and Margie turned the pages of the old book.

4. Which sentence best tells the *theme* of the story?
   - ☐ a. After reading about them in an old book, a girl longs for the schools of the past.
   - ☐ b. It is possible for television to be very educational.
   - ☐ c. By reading books you can learn a great deal about what life was like years ago.

LOOKING AT CLOZE. The following questions use the cloze technique to check your reading comprehension. Complete the paragraph by filling in each blank with one of the words listed below. Each word appears in the story. Since there are five words and four blanks, one of the words will not be used.

It is interesting to _____ what
                            1

the school of the future will be like. Will it

be filled with teaching machines and other

_____ devices? Will it contain
            2

fewer or more _____ per student
                        3

than there are now? Will schools be

_____ different then—so
            4

different we might have trouble recognizing

them?

mechanical   insert

teachers

completely   guess

	☐	× 5 =	☐
	NUMBER CORRECT		YOUR SCORE

	☐	× 5 =	☐
	NUMBER CORRECT		YOUR SCORE

LEARNING HOW TO READ CRITICALLY.
The following questions check your critical
thinking skills. Put an *x* in the box next to
each correct answer.

1. Story clues indicate that Margie and her
   friends were taught
   ☐ a. by teachers who traveled from place
       to place.
   ☐ b. in large buildings.
   ☐ c. by machines at home.

2. In the author's world of the future, students
   ☐ a. have many opportunities to discuss
       things with their teachers.
   ☐ b. don't read books but rather see
       telebooks on a screen.
   ☐ c. get to know their teachers very well.

3. Margie probably hated school because
   ☐ a. she was a very poor student.
   ☐ b. she found it lonely and boring.
   ☐ c. the other students didn't like her.

4. We may conclude that Margie thought
   that the old book was
   ☐ a. ridiculous.
   ☐ b. dull compared to the programs she
       usually watched.
   ☐ c. so interesting that she could hardly
       put it down.

Improving Writing and Discussion Skills

- "The Fun They Had" was written
  more than forty years ago. Do you
  find this surprising? Why?
- What warning does the author seem
  to be offering about schools of the
  future? Explain why you agree or
  disagree with his view. Do you think
  that our system of education will ever
  be like the one described in the story?
  Give reasons to support your opinion.
- It has been said that "television is
  the literature of the future." What
  does this mean? Do you agree? Do
  you approve? Express your ideas on
  the subject in a short essay entitled,
  "Television As the Literature of the
  Future."

Use the boxes below to total your scores
for the exercises. Then write your score on
pages 135 and 136.

☐
+ **S**ELECTING DETAILS FROM THE STO

☐
+ **K**NOWING NEW VOCABULARY WORD

☐
+ **I**DENTIFYING STORY ELEMENTS

☐
+ **L**OOKING AT CLOZE

☐
▼ **L**EARNING HOW TO READ CRITICAL

☐ **S**core Total: Story 10

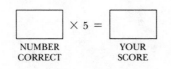

☐ × 5 = ☐

NUMBER   YOUR
CORRECT   SCORE

11. Lonesome Boy

by Arna Bontemps

Meet the Author

Arna Bontemps (1902–1973) was born in Alexandria, Louisiana. For more than twenty years he was a librarian at Fisk University where he also taught. Bontemps was one of the leaders of a group of African-American writers and artists who worked in Harlem, New York City, in the 1920s during what was known as the Harlem Renaissance. Bontemps wrote short stories, plays, poetry, novels, and biographies. He is the author of *Free at Last: The Life of Frederick Douglass* and edited *American Negro Poetry*.

*W*hen Bubber first learned to play the trumpet, his old grandpa winked his eye and laughed.

"You better mind how you blow that horn, sonny boy. You better mind."

"I like to blow loud, I like to blow fast, and I like to blow high," Bubber answered. "Listen to this, Grandpa." And he went on blowing with his eyes closed.

When Bubber was a little bigger, he began carrying his trumpet around with him wherever he went, so his old grandpa scratched his whiskers, took the corncob pipe out of his mouth, and laughed again.

"You better mind *where* you blow that horn, boy," he warned. "I used to blow one myself, and I know."

Bubber smiled. "Where did you ever blow music, Grandpa?"

"Down in New Orleans and all up and down the river. I blowed trumpet most everywhere in my younger days, and I tell you, you better mind where you go blowing."

"I like to blow my trumpet in the school band when it marches, I like to blow it on the landing when the riverboats come in sight, and I like to blow it among the trees in the swamp," he said, still smiling. But when he looked at his grandpa again, he saw a worried look on the old man's face, and he asked, "What's the matter, Grandpa, ain't that all right?"

Grandpa shook his head. "I wouldn't do it if I was you."

That sounded funny to Bubber, but he was not in the habit of disputing his grandfather. Instead he said, "I don't believe I ever heard you blow the trumpet, Grandpa. Don't you want to try blowing on mine now?"

Again the old man shook his head. "My blowing days are long gone," he said. "I still got the lip, but I ain't got the teeth. It takes good teeth to blow high notes on a horn, and these I got ain't much good. They're store teeth."

That made Bubber feel sorry for his grandfather, so he whispered softly, "I'll mind where I blow my horn, Grandpa."

He didn't really mean it though. He just said it to make his grandpa feel good. And the very next day he was half a mile out in the country blowing his horn in a cornfield. Two or three evenings later he was blowing it on a shady lane when the sun went down and not paying much attention where he went.

When he came home, his grandpa met him. "I heard you blowing your horn a long ways away," he said. "The air was still. I could hear it easy."

"How did it sound, Grandpa?"

"Oh, it sounded right pretty." He paused a moment, knocking the ashes out of his pipe, before adding, "Sounded like you mighta been lost."

That made Bubber ashamed of himself, because he knew he had not kept his word and that he was not minding where he blowed his trumpet. "I know what you mean, Grandpa," he answered. "But I can't do like you say. When I'm blowing my horn, I don't always look where I'm going."

Grandpa walked to the window and looked out. While he was standing there, he hitched his overalls up a little higher. He took a red handkerchief from his pocket and wiped his forehead. "Sounded to me like you might have been past Barbin's Landing."

"I was lost," Bubber admitted.

"You can end up in some funny places when you're just blowing a horn and not paying attention. I know," Grandpa insisted. "I know."

"Well, what do you want me to do, Grandpa?"

The old man struck a kitchen match on the seat of his pants and lit a kerosene lamp because the room was black dark by now. While the match was still burning, he lit his pipe. Then he sat down and stretched out his feet. Bubber was on the stool on the other side of the room, his trumpet under his arm. "When you go to school and play your horn in the band, that's all right," the old man said. "When you come home, you ought to put it in the case and leave it there. It ain't good to go traipsing around with a horn in your hand. You might get into devilment."

"But I feel lonesome without my trumpet, Grandpa," Bubber pleaded. "I don't like to go around without it anytime. I feel lost."

Grandpa sighed. "Well, there you are—

lost with it and lost without it. I don't know what's going to become of you, sonny boy."

"You don't understand, Grandpa. You don't understand."

The old man smoked his pipe quietly for a few minutes and then went off to bed, but Bubber did not move. Later on, however, when he heard his grandpa snoring in the next room, he went outdoors, down the path, and around the smokehouse, and sat on a log. The night was still. He couldn't hear anything louder than a cricket. Soon he began wondering how his trumpet would sound on such a still night, back there behind the old smokehouse, so he put the mouthpiece to his lips very lightly and blew a few silvery notes. Immediately Bubber felt better. Now he knew for sure that Grandpa didn't understand how it was with a boy and a horn—a lonesome boy with a silver trumpet. Bubber lifted his horn toward the stars and let the music pour out.

Presently a big orange moon rose, and everything Bubber could see changed suddenly. The moon was so big it made the smokehouse and the trees and the fences seem small. Bubber blew his trumpet loud, he blew it fast, and he blew it high, and in just a few minutes he forgot all about Grandpa sleeping in the house.

He was afraid to talk to Grandpa after that. He was afraid Grandpa might scold him or warn him or try in some other way to persuade him to leave his trumpet in its case. Bubber was growing fast now. He knew what he liked, and he did not think he needed any advice from Grandpa.

Still he loved his grandfather very much, and he had no intention of saying anything that would hurt him. Instead he decided to leave home. He did not tell Grandpa what he was going to do. He just waited till the old man went to sleep in his bed one night. Then he quietly blew out the lamp, put his trumpet under his arm, and started walking down the road from Marksville to Barbin's Landing.

No boat was there, but Bubber did not mind. He knew one would come by before morning, and he knew that he wouldn't be lonesome so long as he had his trumpet with him. He found a place on the little dock where he could lean back against a post and swing his feet over the edge while playing, and the time passed swiftly. And when he finally went aboard a riverboat, just before morning, he found a place on the deck that suited him just as well and went right on blowing his horn.

Nobody asked him to pay any fare. The riverboat men did not seem to expect it of a boy who blew a trumpet the way Bubber did. And in New Orleans the cooks in the kitchens where he ate and the people who kept the rooming houses where he slept did not seem to expect him to pay either. In fact, people seemed to think that a boy who played a trumpet where the patrons of a restaurant could hear him or for the guests of a rooming house should receive money for it. They began to throw money around Bubber's feet as he played his horn.

At first he was surprised. Later he decided it only showed how wrong Grandpa had been about horn blowing. So he picked up all the money they threw, bought himself fancy new clothes, and began looking for new places to play. He ran into boys who played guitars or bull fiddles or drums or other instruments, and he played right along with them. He went out with them to play for picnics or barbecues or boat excursions or dances. He played early in the morning and he played late at night, and he bought new clothes and dressed up so fine he scarcely knew himself in a mirror. He scarcely knew day from night.

It was wonderful to play the trumpet like that, Bubber thought, and to make all that money. People telephoned to the rooming house where he lived and asked for him nearly every day. Some sent notes asking if he would play his trumpet at their parties. Occasionally one would send an automobile to bring him to the place, and this was the best of all. Bubber liked riding through the pretty part of the city to the ballrooms in which well-dressed people waited to dance to his music. He enjoyed even more the times when he was taken to big white-columned houses in the country, houses surrounded by old trees with moss on them.

But he went to so many places to play his trumpet, he forgot where he had been and he got into the habit of not paying much attention. That was how it was the day he received a strange call on the telephone. A voice that sounded like a very proper gentleman said, "I would like to speak to the boy from Marksville, the one who plays the trumpet."

"I'm Bubber, sir, I'm the one."

"Well, Bubber, I'm having a very special party tonight—very special," the voice said. "I want you to play for us."

Bubber felt a little drowsy because he had been sleeping when the phone rang, and he still wasn't too wide awake. He yawned as he answered, "Just me, sir? You want me to play by myself?"

"There will be other musicians, Bubber. You'll play in the band. We'll be looking for you?"

"Where do you live, sir?" Bubber asked sleepily.

"Never mind about that, Bubber. I'll send my chauffeur with my car. He'll bring you."

The voice was growing faint by this time, and Bubber was not sure he caught the last words. "Where did you say, sir?" he asked suddenly. "When is it you want me?"

"I'll send my chauffeur," the voice repeated and then faded out completely.

Bubber put the phone down and went back to his bed to sleep some more. He had played his trumpet very late the night before, and now he just couldn't keep his eyes open.

Something was ringing when he woke up again. Was it the telephone? Bubbler jumped out of bed and ran to answer, but the phone buzzed when he put it to his ear. There was nobody on the line. Then he knew it must have been the doorbell. A moment later he heard the door open, and footsteps came down the dark hall toward Bubber's room. Before Bubber could turn on the light, the footsteps were just outside his room, and a man's voice said, "I'm the chauffeur. I've brought the car to take you to the dance."

"So soon?" Bubber asked, surprised.

The man laughed. "You must have slept all day. It's night now, and we have a long way to drive."

"I'll put on my clothes," Bubber said.

The street light was shining through the window, so he did not bother to switch on the light in his room. Bubber never liked to open his eyes with a bright light shining, and anyway he knew right where to put his hands on the clothes he needed. As he began slipping into them, the chauffeur turned away. "I'll wait for you at the curb," he said.

"All right," Bubber called. "I'll hurry."

When he finished dressing, Bubber took his trumpet off the shelf, closed the door of his room, and went out to where the tall driver was standing beside a long, shiny automobile. The chauffeur saw him coming and opened the door to the back seat. When Bubber stepped in, he threw a lap robe across his knees and closed the door. Then the chauffeur went around to his place in the front seat, stepped on the starter, switched on his headlights, and sped away.

The car was finer than any Bubber had ridden in before; the motor purred so softly and the chauffeur drove it so smoothly, that Bubber soon began to feel sleepy again. One thing puzzled him, however. He had not yet seen the driver's face, and he wondered what the man looked like. But now the chauffeur's cap was down so far over his eyes and his coat collar was turned up so high Bubber could not see his face at all, no matter how far he leaned forward.

After a while he decided it was no use. He would have to wait till he got out of the car to look at the man's face. In the meantime he would sleep. Bubber pulled the lap robe up over his shoulders, stretched out on the wide back seat of the car and went to sleep again.

The car came to a stop, but Bubber did not wake up till the chauffeur opened the door and touched his shoulder. When he stepped out of the car, he could see nothing but dark, twisted trees with moss hanging from them. It was a dark and lonely place, and Bubber was so surprised he did not remember to look at the chauffeur's face. Instead, he followed the tall figure up a path covered with leaves to a white-columned house with lights shining in the windows.

Bubber felt a little better when he saw the big house with the bright windows. He had played in such houses before, and he was glad for a chance to play in another. He took his trumpet from under his arm, put the mouthpiece to his lips, and blew a few bright, clear notes as he walked. The chauffeur did not turn around. He led Bubber to a side entrance, opened the door, and pointed the boy to the room where the dancing had already started. Without ever showing his face, the chauffeur closed the door and returned to the car.

Nobody had to tell Bubber what to do now. He found a place next to the big fiddle that made the rhythms, waited a moment for the beat, then came in with his trumpet. With the bass fiddle, the drums, and the other stringed instruments backing him up, Bubber began to bear down on his trumpet. This was just what he liked. He played loud, he played fast, he played high, and it was all he could do to keep from laughing when he thought about Grandpa and remembered how the old man had told him to mind how he played his horn. Grandpa should see him now, Bubber thought.

Bubber looked at the dancers swirling on the ballroom floor under the high swinging chandelier, and he wished that Grandpa could somehow be at the window and see how they glided and spun around to the music of his horn. He wished the old man could get at least one glimpse of the handsome dancers, the beautiful women in bright-colored silks, the slender men in black evening clothes.

As the evening went on, more people came and began dancing. The floor became more and more crowded, and Bubber played louder and louder, faster and faster, and by midnight the gay ballroom seemed to be spinning like a pinwheel. The floor looked like glass under the dancers' feet. The drapes on the windows resembled gold, and Bubber was playing his trumpet so hard and so fast his eyes looked like they were ready to pop out of his head.

But he was not tired. He felt as if he could go on playing like this forever. He did not even need a short rest. When the other musicians called for a break and went outside to catch a breath of fresh air, he kept right on blowing his horn, running up the scale and down, hitting high C's, swelling out on the notes and then letting them fade away. He kept the dancers entertained till the full band came back, and he blew the notes that started them to dancing again.

Bubber gave no thought to the time, and when a breeze began blowing through the tall windows, he paid no attention. He played as loud as ever, and the dancers swirled just as fast. But there was one thing that did bother him a little. The faces of the dancers began to look thin and hollow as the breeze brought streaks and morning mist into the room. What was the matter with them? Were they tired from dancing all night? Bubber wondered.

But the morning breeze blew stronger and stronger. The curtains flapped, and a gray light appeared in the windows. By this time Bubber noticed that the people who were dancing had no faces at all, and though they continued to dance wildly as he played his trumpet, they seemed dim and far away. Were they disappearing?

Soon Bubber could scarcely see them at all. Suddenly he wondered where the party had gone. The musicians too grew dim and finally disappeared. Even the room with the big chandelier and the golden drapes on the windows was fading away like a techni-color dream. Bubber was frightened when he realized that nothing was left, and he was

alone. Yes, definitely, he was alone—but *where?* Where was he now?

He never stopped blowing his shiny trumpet. In fact, as the party began to break up in this strange way, he blew harder than ever to help himself feel brave again. He also closed his eyes. That was why he happened to notice how uncomfortable the place where he was sitting had become. It was about as unpleasant as sitting on a log. And it was while his eyes were closed that he first became aware of leaves nearby, leaves rustling and blowing in the cool breeze.

But he could not keep his eyes closed for long with so much happening. Bubber just had to peep eventually, and when he did, he saw only leaves around him. Certainly leaves were nothing to be afraid of, he thought, but it was a little hard to understand how the house and room in which he had been playing for the party all night had been replaced by branches and leaves like this. Bubber opened both his eyes wide, stopped blowing his horn for a moment, and took a good, careful look at his surroundings.

Only then did he discover for sure that he was not in a house at all. There were no dancers, no musicians, nobody at all with him, and what had seemed like a rather uncomfortable chair or log was a large branch. Bubber was sitting in a pecan tree, and now he realized that this was where he had been blowing his trumpet so fast and so loud and so high all night. It was very discouraging.

But where was the chauffeur who had brought him here and what had become of the party and the graceful dancers? Bubber climbed down and began looking around. He could see no trace of the things that had seemed so real last night, so he decided he had better go home. Not home to the rooming house where he slept while in New Orleans, but home to the country where Grandpa lived.

He carried his horn under his arm, but he did not play a note on the bus that took him back to Marksville next day. And when he got off the bus and started walking down the road to Grandpa's house in the country, he still didn't feel much like playing anything on his trumpet.

Grandpa was sleeping in a hammock under a chinaberry tree when he arrived, but he slept with one eye open, so Bubber did not have to wake him up. He just stood there, and Grandpa smiled.

"I looked for you to come home before now," the old man said.

"I should have come home sooner," Bubber answered, shamefaced.

"I expected you to be blowing on your horn when you came."

"That's what I want to talk to you about, Grandpa."

The old man sat up in the hammock and put his feet on the ground. He scratched his head and reached for his hat. "Don't tell me anything startling," he said. "I just woke up, and I don't want to be surprised so soon."

Bubber thought maybe he should not mention what had happened. "All right, Grandpa," he whispered, looking rather sad. He leaned against the chinaberry tree, holding the trumpet under his arm, and waited for Grandpa to speak again.

Suddenly the old man blinked his eyes as if remembering something he had almost forgotten. "Did you mind how you blew on that horn down in New Orleans?" he asked.

"Sometimes I did. Sometimes I *didn't*," Bubber confessed.

Grandpa looked hurt. "I hate to hear that, sonny boy," he said. "Have you been playing your horn at barbecues and boat rides and dances and all such as that?"

"Yes, Grandpa," Bubber said, looking at the ground.

"Keep on like that and you're apt to wind up playing for a devil's ball."

Bubber nodded sadly. "Yes, I know."

Suddenly the old man stood up and put his hand on Bubber's shoulder. "Did a educated gentleman call you on the telephone?"

"He talked so proper I could hardly make out what he was saying."

"Did the chauffeur come in a long shiny car?"

Bubber nodded again. "I ended up in a pecan tree," he told Grandpa.

"I tried to tell you, Bubber, but you wouldn't listen to me."

"I'll listen to you from now on, Grandpa."

Grandpa laughed through his whiskers. "Well, take your trumpet in the house and put it on the shelf while I get you something to eat," he said.

Bubber smiled too. He was hungry, and he had not tasted any of Grandpa's cooking for a long time.

SELECTING DETAILS FROM THE STORY.
The following questions help you check your
reading comprehension. Put an *x* in the box
next to each correct answer.

1. Grandpa advised Bubber to be careful
   about
   - ☐ a. leaving his trumpet in school.
   - ☐ b. the kind of music he played.
   - ☐ c. where he played the trumpet.

2. Grandpa could no longer play the trumpet
   because he
   - ☐ a. didn't have the lip for it.
   - ☐ b. didn't have the good teeth that
     playing it required.
   - ☐ c. got out of breath whenever he blew it.

3. With the money that he got for playing
   the trumpet, Bubber bought
   - ☐ a. new clothes.
   - ☐ b. a shiny automobile.
   - ☐ c. a guitar and some drums.

4. At the end of the story, the dancers and
   the musicians
   - ☐ a. congratulated Bubber and wished
     him well.
   - ☐ b. invited Bubber to play at another
     party.
   - ☐ c. seemed to grow dim and
     disappeared.

KNOWING NEW VOCABULARY WORDS. The
following questions check your vocabulary
skills. Put an *x* in the box next to each correct
answer.

1. Because he loved his grandfather very
   much, Bubber had no intention of
   saying anything that would hurt him.
   Which of the following best defines the
   word *intention*?
   - ☐ a. purpose or plan
   - ☐ b. worry or trouble
   - ☐ c. astonishment or surprise

2. The chauffeur brought the car to take
   Bubber to the dance. A *chauffeur* is a
   - ☐ a. musician.
   - ☐ b. mechanic.
   - ☐ c. driver.

3. People thought that guests in a rooming
   house or patrons of a restaurant should
   pay Bubber for playing his trumpet. As
   used here, the word *patrons* means
   - ☐ a. customers.
   - ☐ b. waiters.
   - ☐ c. performers.

4. Grandpa thought that Bubber should leave
   his trumpet at home because it wasn't
   good "to go traipsing around with a horn
   in your hand." What is the meaning of
   the word *traipsing*?
   - ☐ a. shouting loudly
   - ☐ b. wandering aimlessly
   - ☐ c. shopping foolishly

☐ × 5 = ☐

NUMBER   YOUR
CORRECT   SCORE

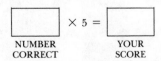

NUMBER   YOUR
CORRECT   SCORE

IDENTIFYING STORY ELEMENTS. The following questions check your knowledge of story elements. Put an *x* in the box next to each correct answer.

1. Who is the *main character* in "Lonesome Boy"?
   - ☐ a. Grandpa
   - ☐ b. Bubber
   - ☐ c. one of the musicians at the party

2. What happened last in the *plot* of the story?
   - ☐ a. Bubber waited for a boat at Barbin's Landing.
   - ☐ b. Bubber found himself sitting in a pecan tree.
   - ☐ c. Bubber was invited to play at a very special party.

3. Which statement best *characterizes* Grandpa?
   - ☐ a. He was very concerned about Bubber.
   - ☐ b. He didn't care about what happened to Bubber.
   - ☐ c. He was jealous because Bubber played the trumpet so well.

4. "Lonesome Boy" is *set*
   - ☐ a. aboard a riverboat.
   - ☐ b. in a theater in New York City.
   - ☐ c. in and around New Orleans.

LOOKING AT CLOZE. The following questions use the cloze technique to check your reading comprehension. Complete the paragraph by filling in each blank with one of the words listed below. Each word appears in the story. Since there are five words and four blanks, one of the words will not be used.

By the age of seventeen, Louis ("Satchmo")

Armstrong was one of the jazz "trumpet

kings" of New _____, his home
                        1

town. By twenty-five, he was a well-known

recording star and _____.
                              2

Armstrong was famous for the beautiful tone

he produced on the _____.
                              3

But his gruff, husky singing voice also

_____ millions.
          4

musician   Orleans

disputing

entertained   trumpet

	× 5 =	
NUMBER CORRECT		YOUR SCORE

	× 5 =	
NUMBER CORRECT		YOUR SCORE

LEARNING HOW TO READ CRITICALLY.
The following questions check your critical
thinking skills. Put an *x* in the box next to
each correct answer.

1. Story clues indicate that Grandpa
   had once
   ☐ a. had an experience similar to
      Bubber's.
   ☐ b. been a rich and famous trumpet
      player.
   ☐ c. received the same advice he gave
      to Bubber.

2. Which statement is true?
   ☐ a. Bubber always followed his
      grandfather's suggestions.
   ☐ b. When Bubber played the trumpet,
      he didn't feel lonesome.
   ☐ c. Most people didn't care for the way
      Bubber played the trumpet.

3. Clues in the story suggest that the dancers
   at the party were
   ☐ a. wealthy people who lived in the area.
   ☐ b. friends of Bubber's grandfather.
   ☐ c. ghosts or ghostly creatures.

4. The story makes the point that
   ☐ a. Bubber should have listened to his
      grandfather.
   ☐ b. few people appreciate good music.
   ☐ c. Bubber will be a professional
      musician one day.

☐ × 5 = ☐

NUMBER   YOUR
CORRECT   SCORE

Improving Writing and Discussion Skills

- On the way to the party, Bubber
  realized that the driver's "cap was
  down so far over his eyes and his coat
  collar was turned up so high Bubber
  could not see his face at all, no matter
  how far he leaned forward." Why do
  you think the author made sure that
  Bubber could not see the driver's face?
- When the dance drew to a close,
  Bubber felt frightened, uncomfortable,
  and uneasy. Explain why in detail.
- Suppose you were telling a friend
  about "Lonesome Boy." How would
  you describe the mood of the story?
  Why do you think the author had
  Bubber go to New Orleans rather than
  some other city?

Use the boxes below to total your scores
for the exercises. Then write your score on
pages 135 and 136.

☐ **S**ELECTING DETAILS FROM THE STOR
+
☐ **K**NOWING NEW VOCABULARY WORDS
+
☐ **I**DENTIFYING STORY ELEMENTS
+
☐ **L**OOKING AT CLOZE
+
☐ **L**EARNING HOW TO READ CRITICALL
▼
☐ **S**core Total: Story 11

12. My Father Goes to Court

by Carlos Bulosan

When I was four, I lived with my mother and brothers and sisters in a small town on the island of Luzon. Father's farm had been destroyed by one of our sudden Philippine floods, so for several years afterward we all lived in the town, though he preferred living in the country. We had as a next-door neighbor a very rich man, whose sons and daughters seldom came out of the house. While we boys and girls played and sang in the sun, his children stayed inside and kept the windows closed. His house was so tall that his children could look in the windows of our house and watch us as we played, or slept, or ate, when there was any food in the house *to* eat.

Now, this rich man's servants were always frying and cooking something good, and the aroma of the food wafted down to us from the windows of the big house. We hung about and took in all the wonderful smells of the food. Sometimes, in the morning, our whole family stood outside the windows of

Meet the Author

Carlos Bulosan (1913–1956) was born in the Philippines, not far from the island of Luzon. While in a hospital recovering from a serious illness, he decided to become a writer. Although Bulosan wrote short stories, articles, poems, and books, his best-known work is *America Is in the Heart,* a true account of his experiences as a migrant worker on the West Coast of the United States. "My Father Goes to Court" is from *The Laughter of My Father.*

103

the rich man's house and listened to the musical sizzling of thick strips of bacon or ham. I can remember one afternoon when our neighbor's servants roasted three chickens. The chickens were young and tender and the fat that dripped into the burning coals gave off an enchanting odor. We watched the servants turn the beautiful birds, and we inhaled the heavenly smell that drifted out to us.

Some days the rich man appeared at a window and glowered down at us. He looked at us one by one, as though he were condemning us. We were all healthy because we went out in the sun every day and bathed in the cool water of the river that flowed from the mountains into the sea. Sometimes we wrestled with one another in the house before we went out to play. We were always in the best of spirits and our laughter was contagious. Other neighbors who passed by our house often stopped in our yard and joined us in laughter.

Laughter was our only wealth. Father was a laughing man. He would go into the living room and stand in front of the tall mirror, stretching his mouth into weird, grotesque shapes with his fingers and making faces at himself. Then he would rush into the kitchen, roaring with laughter.

There was always plenty to make us laugh. There was, for instance, the day one of my brothers came home with a small bundle under his arm, pretending that he had brought something good to eat, maybe a leg of lamb, or something as wonderful as that, which made our mouths water. He rushed to Mother and threw the bundle into her lap. We all stood around watching Mother undo the complicated strings. When she finished, a cat leaped out of the bundle and ran around the house. Mother chased my brother and beat him with her little fist while the rest of us bent over double, choking with laughter.

We made so much noise that all our neighbors except the rich family ran into the yard and joined us in loud, genuine laughter.

It was like that for years.

As time went on, the rich man's children became thin and pale, while we grew even more robust and full of life. Our faces were bright and rosy, but theirs were sad and drawn. The rich man started to cough at night; then he coughed day and night. His wife began coughing too. Then the children started to cough, one after the other. At night their coughing sounded like the barking of a herd of seals. We hung outside the windows and listened to them. We wondered what had happened. We knew that they were not sick from lack of nourishing food, because they were always frying something delicious to eat.

One day the rich man appeared at the window and stood there for a long time. He looked at my sisters, who had grown strong with laughing, then at my brothers, whose arms and legs were like the *molave*, which is the sturdiest tree in the Philippines. He slammed down the window and ran through his house, shutting all the windows.

From that day on, the windows of my neighbor's house were always closed. The children did not come outdoors anymore. We could still hear the servants cooking in the kitchen, and no matter how tightly the windows were shut, the aroma of the food came to us in the wind and drifted on the air into our house.

One morning a police officer came to our house with a sealed paper. The rich man had filed a complaint against us. Father took me with him when he went to the town clerk and asked him what it was about. The clerk told Father that the rich man claimed that for years we had been stealing the smell of his food.

Finally the day came for us to appear in court. We were the first to arrive. Father sat on a chair in the center of the courtroom. Mother occupied a chair by the door. We children sat on a long bench by the wall. Father kept jumping up from his chair and stabbing the air with his arms, as though he were defending himself before an imaginary jury.

The rich man arrived. He had grown old and feeble; his face was scarred with deep lines. With him was his young lawyer. Spectators came in and filled most of the chairs. The judge entered the room and sat on a tall chair. We stood up at once and then sat down again.

After the young lawyer made his opening statement, the judge looked at Father. "Do you need a lawyer?" he asked.

"I don't need any lawyer, Judge," Father said.

"Proceed," said the judge.

The rich man's lawyer jumped up and pointed his finger at Father. "Do you or do you not agree that you have been stealing the smell of the complainant's[1] food?"

"I do not!" Father said.

"Do you or do you not agree that while the complainant's servants cooked and fried lamb or chicken, you and your family hung outside his windows and breathed in the heavenly smell of the food?"

"I agree," Father said.

_____
1. **complainant:** a person who makes a complaint in a court of law.

"How do you account for that?"

Father got up and paced around, scratching his head thoughtfully. Then he said, "I would like to see the children of the complainant, Judge."

"Bring in the children of the complainant."

They came in shyly. The spectators covered their mouths with their hands, for they were amazed to see the children so thin and pale. The children walked silently to a bench and sat down without looking up. They stared at the floor and moved their hands uneasily.

Father could not say anything at first. He just stood by his chair and looked at them. Finally he said, "I should like to cross-examine the complainant."

"Proceed."

Father looked at the rich man, then asked, "Do you claim that we _stole_ the smell of your food by hanging outside your windows when the servants cooked it?"

"Yes."

"Then we are going to _pay_ you right now," Father said. He walked over to where we children were sitting on the bench and took my straw hat off my lap. He dropped into it some coins that he took out of his pocket. He went to Mother, who added a handful of coins. My brothers and sisters threw in their small change too.

"May I walk to the room across the hall for a moment, Judge?" Father asked.

"As you wish," said the judge.

"Thank you," Father said. He strode into the room across the hall with the hat in his hands. It was almost full of coins. The doors of both rooms were wide open.

"Are you ready?" Father called.

"Proceed," the judge said.

Father shook the hat. The sweet tinkle of the coins carried into the courtroom. The spectators turned their faces toward the sound with wonder. Father came back and stood before the complainant.

"Did you hear it?" asked Father.

"Hear what?" the man asked.

"The sound of the money when I shook this hat?" he asked.

"Yes."

"Then you are paid," Father said. "I have paid for the *smell* of the food with the *sound* of the money."

The rich man opened his mouth to speak but no words came out. The lawyer tried to protest, but the judge pounded his heavy wooden hammer on the desk.

"Case dismissed!" he said.

Father smiled to the spectators around the courtroom. The judge even came down from his chair to shake hands with him.

My sister started laughing. The rest of us followed with our rich, contagious laughter, and soon all of the spectators were doubled up with laughter. And the laughter of the judge was the loudest of all.

SELECTING DETAILS FROM THE STORY.
The following questions help you check your reading comprehension. Put an *x* in the box next to each correct answer.

1. The rich man's sons and daughters
   - ☐ a. seldom came out of the house.
   - ☐ b. often played out of doors.
   - ☐ c. liked to bathe in the nearby river.

2. The rich man accused the Bulosans of stealing
   - ☐ a. several chickens.
   - ☐ b. the smell of his food.
   - ☐ c. a handful of coins.

3. Father paid the rich man by giving him
   - ☐ a. some small change.
   - ☐ b. a hatful of cash.
   - ☐ c. the sound of money.

4. At the end of the story, the judge
   - ☐ a. dismissed the case.
   - ☐ b. told Father to hire a lawyer.
   - ☐ c. ruled in favor of the rich man.

KNOWING NEW VOCABULARY WORDS.
The following questions check your vocabulary skills. Put an *x* in the box next to each correct answer.

1. The rich man appeared at the window and glowered down, looking "at us one by one, as though he were condemning us." The word *glowered* means
   - ☐ a. shouted loudly.
   - ☐ b. stared angrily.
   - ☐ c. smiled graciously.

2. Since our laughter was contagious, other neighbors who passed by our house often joined us in laughter. Which of the following best defines the word *contagious*?
   - ☐ a. catching or easily spread
   - ☐ b. very quiet or soft
   - ☐ c. false or untrue

3. Father would stretch his mouth into weird, grotesque shapes with his fingers. What is the meaning of the word *grotesque*?
   - ☐ a. attractive
   - ☐ b. tiny
   - ☐ c. odd

4. The rich man's children became thin and pale, while the neighbors grew robust and full of life. The word *robust* means
   - ☐ a. strong and healthy.
   - ☐ b. weak and tired.
   - ☐ c. poorer and poorer.

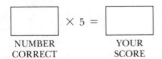

× 5 =

NUMBER CORRECT   YOUR SCORE

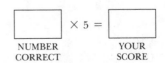

× 5 =

NUMBER CORRECT   YOUR SCORE

IDENTIFYING STORY ELEMENTS. The following questions check your knowledge of story elements. Put an *x* in the box next to each correct answer.

1. Who is the *narrator* of "My Father Goes to Court"?
   - ☐ a. the judge
   - ☐ b. Father
   - ☐ c. the writer, Carlos Bulosan

2. "My Father Goes to Court" is *set* in a
   - ☐ a. small town on the island of Luzon some years ago.
   - ☐ b. village in the United States.
   - ☐ c. large city in France at the present time.

3. Father's family is best *characterized* as
   - ☐ a. wealthy but friendly.
   - ☐ b. timid and quiet.
   - ☐ c. poor, happy, and healthy.

4. What was the author's *purpose* in writing the story?
   - ☐ a. to shock or frighten the reader
   - ☐ b. to entertain or amuse the reader
   - ☐ c. to change the reader's mind

LOOKING AT CLOZE. The following questions use the cloze technique to check your reading comprehension. Complete the paragraph by filling in each blank with one of the words listed below. Each word appears in the story. Since there are five words and four blanks, one of the words will not be used.

Situated in the western Pacific Ocean, the Republic of the _____ consists
1

of over 7,100 islands. More than half of these

_____ are less than a square
2

mile in area and do not have names. The

largest island, _____ , in the
3

north, is nearly 41,000 square miles in size.

Its physical features include many excellent

harbors and tall, rugged _____ .
4

imaginary   mountains

Luzon

islands   Philippines

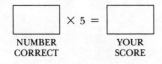

NUMBER CORRECT × 5 = YOUR SCORE

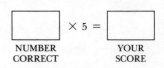

NUMBER CORRECT × 5 = YOUR SCORE

LEARNING HOW TO READ CRITICALLY.
The following questions check your critical
thinking skills. Put an *x* in the box next to
each correct answer.

1. We may infer that the rich man's children
   didn't get enough
   ☐ a. exercise.
   ☐ b. food.
   ☐ c. toys.

2. It is likely that the rich man was angry
   at Father because the Bulosans
   ☐ a. had been stealing from him.
   ☐ b. were so healthy that the rich man
       envied them.
   ☐ c. had often complained about him
       to their neighbors.

3. When Father saw the rich man's children,
   he "could not say anything at first. He
   just stood by his chair and looked at
   them." Father was probably
   ☐ a. too angry at them to say anything.
   ☐ b. surprised at how much they had
       grown.
   ☐ c. shocked by how sickly they looked.

4. The conclusion of the story suggests that
   the judge was
   ☐ a. very amused by the case.
   ☐ b. relieved that the difficult case
       was over.
   ☐ c. making fun of Father.

Improving Writing and Discussion Skills

- Were you able to guess how the story
  was going to end? What incident
  provides the key clue to what
  eventually happens?
- When do you think Father planned
  his actions—*before* he arrived in court,
  or *after* he made his appearance?
  Explain your answer.
- Suppose you were a reporter assigned
  to cover the case for a local newspaper. Write the news story, including
  as many facts as you can. If you wish,
  make up a headline for your story.

Use the boxes below to total your scores
for the exercises. Then write your score on
pages 135 and 136.

☐
  SELECTING DETAILS FROM THE STORY
  +
☐
  KNOWING NEW VOCABULARY WORDS
  +
☐
  IDENTIFYING STORY ELEMENTS
  +
☐
  LOOKING AT CLOZE
  +
☐
  LEARNING HOW TO READ CRITICALLY
  ▼
☐
  Score Total: Story 12

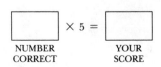

NUMBER ☐ × 5 = ☐ YOUR
CORRECT   SCORE

13. The Piece of String

by Guy de Maupassant

Meet the Author

Guy de Maupassant (1850–1893) is considered one of the world's greatest writers of short stories. Born in Normandy, France, he later settled in Paris. His first story was published when he was thirty years old. With a simple, direct style, he wrote six novels, several travel books, a book of poetry, and sixteen volumes of short stories. Among his most famous stories are "The Necklace," "The Duel," and "The Piece of String."

*A*ll the roads near Goderville were crowded with peasants heading toward the little town because it was market day. The men walked slowly, plodding along, their shoulders hunched forward as they moved. Their bodies had been deformed by long years of hard labor—by the presssure of the plow, by all the endless and strenuous tasks of farming.

Some of the farmers led a cow or a calf by a rope, while their wives, walking behind the animal, whipped its sides with a leafy branch to hurry it along. The women carried large baskets from which protruded, in some cases, the head of a chicken or a duck.

Now and then a wagon, drawn by an old horse, passed by. Its inhabitants, bumping up and down on the rocky road, held tightly to the sides to soften the jolts.

The large square at Goderville was filled with a teeming throng of human beings and animals. Everywhere there was noise—shrill

111

shouting, loud voices, which sometimes was dominated by the robust laugh of a farmer, or by the long mooing sound of a cow.

Mr. Haycorne, from the village of Bréauté, had just arrived at Goderville. He was making his way toward the square when he noticed a small piece of string on the ground. Haycorne, who was very thrifty, thought to himself "anything useful is worth having." So he bent down, though it was painful to do so because his back was bothering him, and picked up the piece of string. He was about to roll it up carefully when he noticed Mr. Malandain standing in the doorway of his shop, looking at him closely. Once they had had a quarrel over the price of a harness. Ever since then they had been on bad terms, for each was the type to hold a grudge forever.

Mr. Haycorne felt a little embarrassed at being seen by his enemy this way, picking a piece of string out of the dirt and mud on the road. Haycorne quickly hid the piece of string under the jacket he was wearing and then slipped it into his trouser pocket. Then he pretended to continue searching the ground, as though looking for something that he could not find. After a while, he continued on his way to the square and within a few moments, he was lost in the noisy, slow-moving crowd.

Everyone there was busy endlessly bargaining. Peasants looked at cows they considered buying. They would prod the cows, walk away, come back, and then study the animals again, unable to make a decision for fear of being cheated.

The women put their large baskets down on the ground and took out the poultry that were tied together by the legs. The women listened to offers for the birds and sometimes asked for more money, or shouted to a customer who was walking away, "All right, I'll let you have it for your price."

Then, little by little, the crowd in the square thinned out. The church bell rang out the hour of noon, and those who lived too far away to go home, went off to the various inns.

At Jourdain's, one popular inn, the large dining room was crowded with customers, while outside the courtyard was filled with wagons and carts of every description.

To the rear of the diners in the inn stood a huge fireplace in which a fire blazed brightly. In the fireplace were three spits on which revolved chickens, pigeons, and legs of mutton. Delicious aromas filled the room, delighting all hearts and making everyone's mouth water. Soon, dishes were served, passed around, and emptied, as were the jugs of yellow cider. Everybody talked about the business that had been done so far, what had been bought and sold and traded. The talk turned to the crops and weather. The rain, it was agreed, was good for the vegetables, a bit too damp for the wheat.

All of a sudden, the heavy roll of a drum sounded in the courtyard in front of the inn. The diners jumped up and ran to the door or to the windows, their mouths still full, their napkins in their hands.

The town crier completed his roll on the drum. Then, in a loud voice, he made the following announcement:

"Let it be hereby known to the inhabitants of Goderville, and in general to all persons present at the market today, that there was lost this morning, on the Beville Road, between nine and ten o'clock, a black leather wallet containing five hundred francs and some business papers. The finder is hereby requested to return the wallet immediately to the mayor's office, or to Mr. Felix Breque of Manneville. A reward of twenty francs will be given to the person who returns it."

Then the man went away. The dull roll of the drum and the faint voice of the town crier were soon heard once again in the distance.

Everyone began talking of this incident, debating how likely it was that the wallet would eventually be returned to Mr. Breque. They were just finishing their coffee, when the chief of police appeared at the door.

He asked, "Is Mr. Haycorne of Bréauté here?"

Mr. Haycorne, who was seated at the far end of the room, replied, "Yes, here I am."

The officer went on: "Mr. Haycorne, would you be good enough to come with me to the town hall? The mayor would like to have a few words with you."

The peasant, surprised and a little uneasy, downed his last swallow of coffee, rose at once, and set off slowly—for his back was quite sore—following the police chief.

The mayor, seated comfortably in a large armchair, was waiting. He was a heavy, solemn man, who took himself very seriously.

"Mr. Haycorne," said the mayor, "you were seen this morning, on the Beville Road, picking up the wallet lost by Felix Breque of Manneville."

The peasant stared in astonishment at the mayor, terrified by this suspicion that had fallen on him without his knowing why.

"Me?" stammered Mr. Haycorne. "Me? You say *I* picked up the wallet?"

"Yes, you, yourself."

"On my word of honor, I never saw it."

"But you were seen."

"I was seen? Me? Who says he saw me?"

"Mr. Malandain, the harness maker."

Then the peasant remembered what had happened. He understood and grew red with rage.

"Ah, so he said he saw me, did he, the dog! He saw me picking up this piece of string here, mayor. Here it is."

And, rummaging in his pocket, he pulled out the string.

But the mayor, who obviously did not believe him, shook his head and said: "You'll never convince me, Mr. Haycorne, that Malandain, who is a man who can be trusted, mistook that piece of string for a wallet."

The peasant, furious, raised his hand as though taking an oath. "But it's the truth," he protested. "It's true! I tell you, it's true!"

The mayor went on calmly, "And after picking up the wallet, you even searched about in the mud for a while to see if any coins had fallen out."

Mr. Haycorne was almost speechless with anger and fear. "How dare he—how dare he—make up lies—lies—to ruin my reputation. How dare he—"

But in spite of all his protests, the mayor did not believe him.

They brought in Malandain, who repeated and stood by his statement. For an hour Haycorne and Malandain hurled insults at each other. At his own request, Haycorne was searched. Nothing was found.

Finally the mayor, not sure of what to do, told Haycorne he could go. "But I warn you," said the mayor, "I will repeat this to the public prosecutor and wait for further instructions."

The news had spread. As he left the town hall, the old man was surrounded by people who questioned him with eager curiosity. He started telling the story of the piece of string. Nobody believed him. Everybody laughed.

As he walked along, other people stopped him, and he stopped friends and acquaintances, telling one and all the story over and over, declaring his innocence, and showing his pockets, which he had turned inside out to prove that he had nothing.

Everybody said, "Come, now, you old rascal."

This proved too much for Haycorne. He lost his temper and became irritated and angry because no one would believe him. But since he didn't know what to do, he just went on endlessly repeating his story.

Finally it grew dark and he had to leave for home. He started on his way with three of his neighbors to whom he had pointed out the spot where he had picked up the string. And all the way home he spoke of nothing but what had happened.

In the evening he wandered around the village of Bréauté in order to tell everyone his story. Nobody believed him.

The next day, about one o'clock in the afternoon, Marius Paumelle, a laborer who worked on a farm at Deauville, returned the wallet and its contents to Felix Breque of Manneville.

The man claimed to have found the object on the road. But as he could not read, he had taken it back to the farm and given it to his employer.

The news spread through the neighborhood and soon reached Mr. Haycorne. He immediately went all around the town telling everyone the story again, this time with its happy ending. He was triumphant.

"What really upset me so much," he said, "wasn't the thing itself, but the *lies*. There's nothing worse than being falsely blamed because of a lie."

He talked about his adventure all day long; he told it to people he met on the road, to people stopping at the inn, to people coming out of church the following Sunday. He even stopped strangers to tell them his story. He felt much better about things now, and yet something was bothering him without his knowing exactly what it was. People seemed to be somewhat amused as they listened to him. They did not seem convinced. He had the feeling that remarks were being made behind his back.

The following Tuesday he went to the market at Goderville simply because he felt the need to tell his story.

Malandain, standing in his doorway, burst out laughing when he saw him go buy. Why?

He stopped a farmer from Criquetot and began to tell him the story. The farmer did not let him finish but gave him a poke in the ribs, saying, "You clever rogue." Then the farmer turned on his heels and walked quickly away.

Haycorne was confused and felt somewhat uneasy. Why had the farmer called him a clever rogue?

He sat down at a table at Jourdain's and began to explain the story again.

A horse dealer from Montivilliers shouted to him, "Get away, you old rascal! I know your little trick with your piece of string."

Haycorne stammered, "But . . . but . . . the wallet was found."

Someone else called out, "Come, come, I know your game. One man finds it and another man brings it back. No one is any the wiser, and you're off the hook."

The peasant was speechless. At last he understood. They were accusing him of getting an accomplice, a helper, to return the wallet.

He tried to protest, but everyone burst out laughing.

He was unable to finish his dinner and went away to the sound of laughter and jeers.

Haycorne returned home ashamed and indignant, angry and confused. He was also upset because he knew that he was so cunning that he was actually capable of doing what he had been accused of— and of boasting of it as a good trick later. Yes, his cleverness was very well known, so that it would be difficult now to prove that he was innocent. Still he was *not* guilty, and the unfairness of the suspicions hurt him deeply.

Then he began to tell the story all over again. He enlarged it every day, adding more and more details that he had spent many hours preparing, and by now he could think of nothing else but the story of the string. And the louder and more vehemently he protested that he was innocent, the more elaborately he defended himself, the less people believed him.

"A good liar knows how to make excuses," people said behind his back.

Haycorne realized this and it preyed upon his heart. He exhausted himself as he tried, without success, to change their minds. Before long he began visibly wasting away.

The local jokers now made him tell the story of the string. As soon as he began, everyone winked with amusement. His mind, seriously weakened, began to give way.

Toward the end of December, Haycorne took to his bed.

He died early in January. In his fever, as he struggled with death, he proclaimed his innocence, repeating over and over:

"A little piece of string . . . a little piece of string . . . see, here it is . . . a little piece of string."

SELECTING DETAILS FROM THE STORY.
The following questions help you check your reading comprehension. Put an x in the box next to each correct answer.

1. The large square at Goderville was filled with people who were
   - ☐ a. on their way to a nearby town.
   - ☐ b. taking a stroll on a beautiful day.
   - ☐ c. buying and selling things.

2. The town crier announced that
   - ☐ a. the mayor wanted to see Mr. Haycorne immediately.
   - ☐ b. a wallet containing five hundred francs had been lost.
   - ☐ c. the chief of police planned to question everyone at the inn.

3. Mr. Malandain said that he saw Haycorne
   - ☐ a. pick a piece of string out of the dirt on the road.
   - ☐ b. get into a quarrel over the price of a harness.
   - ☐ c. pick up a wallet.

4. Eventually Haycorne realized that people thought that he was
   - ☐ a. lying.
   - ☐ b. innocent.
   - ☐ c. misunderstood.

KNOWING NEW VOCABULARY WORDS.
The following questions check your vocabulary skills. Put an x in the box next to each correct answer.

1. The farmers were used to . . . hard labor—to the endless and strenuous tasks of farming. Something that is *strenuous*
   - ☐ a. requires much energy.
   - ☐ b. is easy to do.
   - ☐ c. is soon forgotten.

2. "The women carried large baskets from which protruded, in some cases, the head of a chicken or a duck." The word *protruded* means
   - ☐ a. cried out.
   - ☐ b. rushed out.
   - ☐ c. stuck out.

3. Finally Haycorne understood that he was being accused of "getting an accomplice, a helper, to return the wallet." What is an *accomplice*?
   - ☐ a. a relative one has not seen for years
   - ☐ b. a person who aids another, generally in committing a crime
   - ☐ c. someone who knows the law

4. Haycorne was so cunning that he was actually capable of doing what he was accused of—and his cleverness was well known. Define the word *cunning*.
   - ☐ a. sly
   - ☐ b. foolish
   - ☐ c. humble

	× 5 =	
NUMBER CORRECT		YOUR SCORE

	× 5 =	
NUMBER CORRECT		YOUR SCORE

IDENTIFYING STORY ELEMENTS. The following questions check your knowledge of story elements. Put an *x* in the box next to each correct answer.

1. Which expression best *characterizes* Mr. Haycorne?
   - ☐ a. thrifty and shrewd
   - ☐ b. trusted and respected
   - ☐ c. young and cheerful

2. What happened first in the *plot* of the story?
   - ☐ a. Haycorne's mind weakened and began to fail.
   - ☐ b. A laborer returned the wallet and its contents.
   - ☐ c. Haycorne searched the ground, as if looking for something he could not find.

3. "There's nothing worse than being falsely blamed because of a lie." This line of *dialogue* was spoken by
   - ☐ a. the mayor.
   - ☐ b. Mr. Haycorne.
   - ☐ c. Mr. Malandain.

4. In "The Piece of String" there is *conflict* between
   - ☐ a. Mr. Malandain and the mayor.
   - ☐ b. Mr. Malandain and Mr. Haycorne.
   - ☐ c. Mr. Haycorne and the town crier.

LOOKING AT CLOZE. The following questions use the cloze technique to check your reading comprehension. Complete the paragraph by filling in each blank with one of the words listed below. Each word appears in the story. Since there are five words and four blanks, one of the words will not be used.

The earliest plow was simply a stick that was used to break up the _____ .
1

This crooked-stick plow was _____
2

replaced by wooden plows, generally pulled by oxen. While wooden plows are still used in many places today, _____
3

made of iron and steel are far more efficient. Of course, giant tractor plows are

_____ of digging up many acres
4

of land in a single day.

capable   ground

inhabitants

plows   eventually

☐ × 5 = ☐

NUMBER
CORRECT

YOUR
SCORE

☐ × 5 = ☐

NUMBER
CORRECT

YOUR
SCORE

LEARNING HOW TO READ CRITICALLY.
The following questions check your critical
thinking skills. Put an x in the box next to
each correct answer.

1. We may infer that Haycorne died from
   - ☐ a. an illness caused by the stress
     he suffered.
   - ☐ b. injuries suffered in a fight.
   - ☐ c. a terrible accident in town.

2. Probably, one reason people didn't believe
   Haycorne's story was that
   - ☐ a. Haycorne couldn't provide any
     details about what happened.
   - ☐ b. Haycorne didn't seem very sure
     of himself.
   - ☐ c. it was hard for them to believe that
     someone would bother to pick up
     and save a little piece of string.

3. Which statement is true?
   - ☐ a. The mayor believed that Haycorne
     was telling the truth.
   - ☐ b. Eventually Haycorne became a source
     of amusement to the townspeople.
   - ☐ c. Mr. Malandain saw Haycorne pick
     up a black leather wallet.

4. It is reasonable to conclude that Haycorne
   would have been better off if he had
   - ☐ a. said very little about the piece of
     string after the wallet was returned.
   - ☐ b. claimed he was innocent even more
     vigorously than he did.
   - ☐ c. tried to force Malandain to admit
     that he was wrong.

☐	× 5 =	☐
NUMBER CORRECT		YOUR SCORE

Improving Writing and Discussion Skills

- Do you think that Malandain realized
  that Haycorne had picked up a piece
  of string—or did Malandain really
  believe that Haycorne had found the
  wallet? Give reasons for your answer.
- A character in a play by William
  Shakespeare is said to "protest too
  much." What is the meaning of this
  expression? How does it apply to
  Haycorne? Do you think there
  was *any* way Haycorne could have
  convinced the people of his
  innocence? Explain.
- Irony occurs when something
  happens that is the opposite of what
  might naturally be expected. What
  is both sad and ironic in "The Piece
  of String"?

Use the boxes below to total your scores
for the exercises. Then write your score on
pages 135 and 136.

☐ SELECTING DETAILS FROM THE STO▸
+
☐ KNOWING NEW VOCABULARY WORD▸
+
☐ IDENTIFYING STORY ELEMENTS
+
☐ LOOKING AT CLOZE
+
☐ LEARNING HOW TO READ CRITICAL▸
▼
☐ Score Total: Story 13

118

14. Finding the Way

by Helen Keller

Meet the Author

Helen Keller (1880–1968) lost her hearing and sight after a serious illness when she was about two years old. The account of how she eventually learned to read and write is found in her inspiring autobiography, *The Story of My Life*, from which "Finding the Way" is taken. Keller was born in Tuscumbia, Alabama, and graduated with honors from Radcliffe College when she was twenty-four. The numerous books she wrote have been translated into more than fifty languages.

I was nineteen months old when I fell ill to the sickness that took from me my hearing and my sight. When the illness came, it closed my eyes and ears and rendered me unconscious. The doctors thought that I would not live. Early one morning, however, the fever left me as suddenly and mysteriously as it had come. There was great rejoicing in the family that morning, but no one, not even the doctor, knew that I would never see or hear again.

I still have confused recollections of that illness. I especially remember the tenderness with which my mother tried to soothe me in my waking hours of torment and pain. I remember the agony and bewilderment with which I awoke after tossing, half asleep, all night. I remember turning my eyes, dry

119

and hot, to the wall—away from the light I once loved, the light which came to me dimmer and dimmer each day. But except for these memories, if indeed they are truly memories, it all seems very unreal, like a nightmare. Gradually I got used to the silence and darkness that surrounded me, and I forgot that it had ever been different.

I have been told that at six months I could say, "How do you do?" And, even after my illness, I remembered one of the words I had learned in those early months. The word was "water," and I continued to make the sound "wah-wah" even after all other speech was lost. Fortunately, during the first nineteen months of my life, I had seen green fields, the bright sky, trees and flowers. The darkness that followed could not blot these out completely.

I cannot recall what happened during the first months after my illness. I only know that I sat in my mother's lap or clung to her dress as she went about the house. My hands felt every object and became aware of every motion, and in this way I learned to know many things.

Soon I felt the need to communicate with others, and I began to make crude signs. A shake of the head meant "No" and a nod meant "Yes." A pull meant "Come" and a push meant "Go." Was it bread that I wanted? Then I would imitate the acts of cutting slices and buttering them. If I wanted ice cream for dessert, then I began to shiver, indicating cold. My mother helped me to understand a great deal. Indeed, I owe to her loving wisdom all that was bright and good during my long night.

I knew much of what was going on about me. At five I learned to fold and put away the clean clothes when they were brought from the laundry, and I distinguished my own clothes from the rest. I could tell from the way that my mother and aunt dressed that they were going out, and I often tugged to go along with them. I was always present when there was company, and when the guests got ready to leave, I waved my hand to them, a gesture that I vaguely seemed to remember.

I do not know when I first realized that I was different from other people. However, I had noticed that my mother and friends did not use signs as I did but talked with their mouths. Sometimes I stood between two persons who were talking and touched their lips. I could not understand and was troubled and confused. I moved my lips frantically without any result. This made me so angry at times that I kicked and screamed until I was exhausted.

One day I happened to spill water on my apron, and I spread it out to dry in front of the fire that was flickering in the fireplace in the living room. The apron did not dry quickly enough to suit me, so I came closer and threw it right over the hot ashes. The fire began to blaze, the flames encircled me, and in a moment my clothes were burning. I made a terrified noise that brought my nurse to the rescue. Throwing a blanket over me, she almost suffocated me, but she put out the fire. Except for my hands and hair, I was not badly burned.

Meanwhile, the desire to express myself grew. The few signs I used became less and less adequate. At the same time, my failures to make myself understood were followed by outbursts of passion. I felt as if invisible hands were holding me, and I made frantic efforts to free myself. I struggled fiercely and generally broke down in tears, physically exhausted. If my mother happened to be near, I crept into her arms, too miserable even to remember the cause of my outburst. After a while, the need to communicate became so urgent that these outbursts occurred daily, sometimes hourly.

My parents were deeply grieved and distressed. We lived a long way from any school for the blind or the deaf, and it seemed unlikely that anyone would come to such an out-of-the-way place as Tuscumbia, Alabama, to teach a child who was both deaf and blind. Indeed, my friends and relatives sometimes doubted whether I could be taught.

But when I was about six years old, my father heard of an eye doctor in Baltimore who had been successful in many cases that seemed hopeless. My parents decided at once to take me to Baltimore to see if anything could be done for my eyes.

The journey, which I remember well, was very pleasant. I made friends with many people on the train. One lady gave me a box of shells. My father made holes in these so that I could string them together, and for a long time they kept me happy and contented.

My aunt made a big doll out of towels. It was a comical, shapeless thing, this doll, with no nose, mouth, ears, or eyes—nothing that even the imagination of a child could convert into a face. Curiously enough, the absence of eyes struck me more than all the other defects put together. I pointed this out to everybody repeatedly, but no one seemed able to provide the doll with eyes. A bright idea, however, came to me, and the problem was solved. I tumbled off the seat and searched under it until I found my aunt's cape, which was trimmed with large beads. I pulled two beads off and indicated to her that I wanted her to sew them on my doll. She raised my hand to her eyes in a questioning way, and I nodded enthusiastically. The beads were sewed in the right place and I could hardly contain my joy.

When we arrived in Baltimore, Dr. Chisolm received us kindly, but he could do nothing. He said, however, that I could be educated, and he advised my father to consult Dr. Alexander Graham Bell of Washington, who would be able to give us further information about schools and teachers of deaf or blind children. We went immediately to Washington to see Dr. Bell.

I at once felt the tenderness and sympathy that endeared Dr. Bell to so many. He held me on his knee while I examined his watch, and he made it strike the hour for me. He understood my signs, and I knew it, and liked him very much. But I did not dream that the interview would be the door through which I would pass from darkness into light, and from isolation to friendship, companionship, knowledge, and love.

Dr. Bell suggested that my father write to Mr. Anagnos, director of the Perkins Institute in Boston, and ask him if he had a teacher able to begin my education. This my father did at once, and in a few weeks there came a kind letter from Mr. Anagnos. A teacher had been found!

The most important day I remember in all my life is the one on which my teacher, Anne Mansfield Sullivan, came to me. I am filled with wonder when I consider the enormous contrast between the two lives it connects. It was the third of March 1887, three months before I was seven years old.

On the afternoon of that eventful day, I stood on the porch, waiting anxiously. I guessed, from my mother's signs and from the hurrying to and fro in the house, that something unusual was about to happen. Therefore, I went to the door and went out to the steps.

The afternoon sun penetrated the mass of honeysuckle that covered the porch and fell on my upturned face. My fingers lingered on the familiar leaves and blossoms that had just come forth to greet the spring. I did not know what the future held of marvel or surprise for me. Anger and bitterness had preyed upon me continually for weeks and a deep sense of weariness had followed.

Have you ever been at sea in a dense fog, when it seemed as if a thick wall of darkness shut you in, and the great ship groped her way to shore, while you waited with pounding heart for something to happen? I was like that ship before my education began, only I was without a compass and had no way of knowing how near the harbor was.

"Light! Give me light!" was the wordless cry of my soul. And the light of love shone on me in that very hour.

I felt approaching footsteps. I stretched out my hand, thinking it was my mother. Someone took it, and I was caught up and held close in the arms of Anne Mansfield Sullivan, the person who had come to reveal all things to me and, more than anything else, to love me.

The morning after my teacher arrived, she led me into her room and gave me a doll. After I had played with it a little while, Miss Sullivan slowly spelled into my hand the word "d-o-l-l." I was at once interested in this finger play and tried to imitate it. When I finally succeeded in making the letters correctly, I was filled with childish pleasure and pride. Running downstairs to my mother, I held up my hand and made the letters for *doll.* I did not know that I was spelling a word or

even that words existed. I was simply making my fingers go in monkeylike imitation.

In the days that followed I learned to spell in this uncomprehending way a great many words, among them *pin, hat, cup* and a few verbs like *sit, stand,* and *walk.* But my teacher was with me several weeks before I understood that everything has a name.

One day while I was playing, Miss Sullivan put my new doll *and* my big old rag doll into my lap, spelled "d-o-l-l," and tried to make me understand that "d-o-l-l" applied to both. Earlier in the day we had struggled over the words "m-u-g" and "w-a-t-e-r." Miss Sullivan had tried to impress upon me that "m-u-g" is *mug* and that "w-a-t-e-r" is *water.* But I persisted in continually confusing the two.

In despair, she had dropped the subject for the time, only to take it up again at the first opportunity. I became impatient at her repeated attempts and grabbing the new doll, hurled it to the floor. I was delighted when I felt the fragments of the broken doll at my feet. Neither sorrow nor regret followed my outburst. In the still, dark world in which I lived there was no strong sentiment of tenderness.

I felt my teacher sweep the fragments to one side of the hearth, and I felt satisfied that the cause of my discomfort was removed. She brought me my hat, and I knew I was going out into the warm sunshine. This thought, if a wordless sensation may be called a thought, made me hop and skip with pleasure.

We walked down the path to the well, attracted by the fragrance of the honeysuckle. Someone was pumping water, and my teacher placed my hand under the spout. As the cool stream gushed over one hand, she spelled into the other the word *water,* first slowly, then rapidly. I stood still, my complete attention fixed upon the motions of her fingers.

Suddenly I felt a vague awareness of something forgotten—a thrill of returning thought—and somehow the mystery of language was revealed to me. I knew then that "w-a-t-e-r" meant the wonderful cool something that was flowing over my hand! There were barriers still, it is true, but barriers that could in time be swept away.

I left the well eager to learn. Everything had a name, and each name gave birth to a new thought. As we returned to the house, every object that I touched seemed to quiver with life. That was because I saw everything with the strange, new sight that had come to me.

On entering the door, I remember the doll I had broken. I felt my way to the hearth and picked up the pieces. I tried vainly to put them together. Then my eyes filled with tears, for I realized what I had done, and for the first time I felt sorrow and regret.

I learned a great many new words that day. I do not remember what they all were, but I do know that *mother, father, sister, teacher* were among them—words that were to make the world blossom for me.

It would have been difficult to find a happier child than I was as I lay in my crib at the end of that eventful day and lived over the joys it had brought me. For the first time, I longed for a new day to come!

SELECTING DETAILS FROM THE STORY.
The following questions help you check your
reading comprehension. Put an *x* in the box
next to each correct answer.

1. As the result of a sudden and mysterious
   illness, Helen Keller was unable to
   ☐ a. walk.
   ☐ b. think.
   ☐ c. see or hear.

2. Helen often broke down in tears,
   physically exhausted, because she
   could not
   ☐ a. read books.
   ☐ b. make herself understood.
   ☐ c. go out of doors alone.

3. According to Helen, the most important
   day of her life was the one on which
   ☐ a. Anne Mansfield Sullivan came to
        teach her.
   ☐ b. her family took her to an eye doctor
        in Baltimore.
   ☐ c. she barely escaped being killed in
        a fire.

4. The mystery of language was revealed
   to Helen when she
   ☐ a. imitated making the letters for the
        word *doll.*
   ☐ b. struggled over the word *mud.*
   ☐ c. grasped the meaning of the
        word *water.*

KNOWING NEW VOCABULARY WORDS. The
following questions check your vocabulary
skills. Put an *x* in the box next to each correct
answer.

1. Many years later, Helen still had confused
   recollections of her terrible illness. The
   word *recollections* means
   ☐ a. memories.
   ☐ b. medicines.
   ☐ c. playthings.

2. His tenderness and sympathy endeared
   Dr. Bell to everyone who knew him. What
   is the meaning of the word *endeared*?
   ☐ a. made dear
   ☐ b. troubled greatly
   ☐ c. rejected

3. After Helen hurled the doll to the floor,
   her teacher swept the fragments to one
   side. What are *fragments*?
   ☐ a. silly toys
   ☐ b. broken pieces
   ☐ c. foolish ideas

4. Eventually she passed from darkness into
   light, and from isolation to friendship and
   companionship. As used here, the word
   isolation refers to being
   ☐ a. popular.
   ☐ b. clever.
   ☐ c. alone.

	× 5 =	
NUMBER CORRECT		YOUR SCORE

	× 5 =	
NUMBER CORRECT		YOUR SCORE

IDENTIFYING STORY ELEMENTS. The following questions check your knowledge of story elements. Put an *x* in the box next to each correct answer.

1. "Finding the Way" is *set* in
   - ☐ a. Washington at the present time.
   - ☐ b. Boston recently.
   - ☐ c. Alabama a number of years ago.

2. Who is the *narrator* in "Finding the Way"?
   - ☐ a. Anne Mansfield Sullivan
   - ☐ b. Helen Keller
   - ☐ c. Dr. Alexander Graham Bell

3. What happened last in the *plot* of the story?
   - ☐ a. Anne Sullivan placed Helen's hand under the spout as cool water gushed out.
   - ☐ b. A letter came from Dr. Anagnos saying that a teacher had been found.
   - ☐ c. The nurse threw a blanket over Helen to put out the fire on her clothes.

4. The *mood* of "Finding the Way" is
   - ☐ a. serious.
   - ☐ b. humorous.
   - ☐ c. terrifying.

LOOKING AT CLOZE. The following questions use the cloze technique to check your reading comprehension. Complete the paragraph by filling in each blank with one of the words listed below. Each word appears in the story. Since there are five words and four blanks, one of the words will not be used.

When he was three years old, Louis Braille lost his sight as the _____ of an accident. Later Braille was sent to a school for the blind in Paris where he was _____. While still a young man, Braille developed what is known as the braille system. It uses raised dots on paper as _____. A blind person can read the letters by running his or her _____ over the dots.

educated   result

letters

persisted   fingers

	× 5 =	
NUMBER CORRECT		YOUR SCORE

	× 5 =	
NUMBER CORRECT		YOUR SCORE

LEARNING HOW TO READ CRITICALLY.
The following questions check your critical
thinking skills. Put an *x* in the box next to
each correct answer.

1. Story clues indicate that Helen Keller
   □ a. often complained about her bad luck.
   □ b. never let anything bother her.
   □ c. was very intelligent and determined.

2. If she had not met Anne Sullivan, there
   is a good chance that Helen Keller would
   have
   □ a. regained her hearing and her sight.
   □ b. fallen far short of her potential.
   □ c. learned to read and write on her own.

3. Which statement is true?
   □ a. Anne Sullivan was very discouraged
        at Helen's slow progress.
   □ b. Helen Keller's writing shows great
        admiration for Anne Sullivan.
   □ c. All of Helen's friends and relatives
        were confident that Helen would
        become an excellent student.

4. The last paragraph of the story suggests
   that Helen was
   □ a. eager to face the future.
   □ b. disappointed with her teacher.
   □ c. upset about the events of the day.

Improving Writing and Discussion Skills

- The difficulty in being able to communicate plays a very important part
  in this selection. Find evidence from
  the story to support this statement.
  In your answer explain why it was
  so difficult for Helen to learn to speak.
- Why do you think this selection
  appears in a book about encounters?
  What lesson, or lessons, does the story
  offer?
- Suppose you were Anne Mansfield
  Sullivan. Think about the incident
  at the well. Then describe it briefly
  but vividly.

Use the boxes below to total your scores
for the exercises. Then write your score on
pages 135 and 136.

SELECTING DETAILS FROM THE STO

+

KNOWING NEW VOCABULARY WORD

+

IDENTIFYING STORY ELEMENTS

+

LOOKING AT CLOZE

+

LEARNING HOW TO READ CRITICAL

▼

Score Total: Story 14

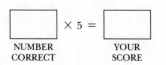

NUMBER   YOUR
CORRECT   SCORE

× 5 =

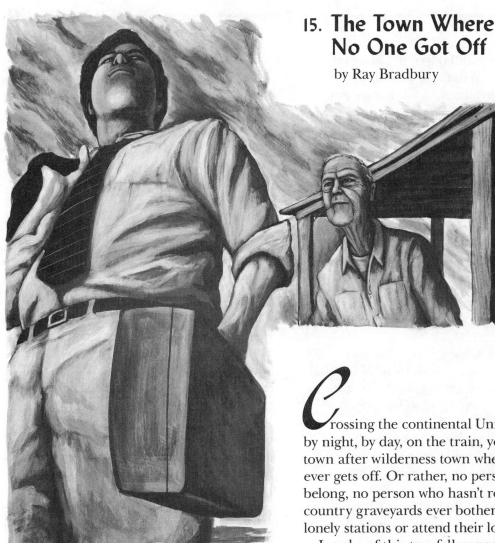

15. The Town Where No One Got Off

by Ray Bradbury

*C*rossing the continental United States by night, by day, on the train, you flash past town after wilderness town where nobody ever gets off. Or rather, no person who doesn't belong, no person who hasn't roots in these country graveyards ever bothers to visit their lonely stations or attend their lonely views.

I spoke of this to a fellow passenger, another salesman like myself, on the Chicago—Los Angeles train as we crossed Iowa.

"True," he said. "People get off in Chicago; everyone gets off there. People get off in New York, get off in Boston, get off in L.A. People who don't live there go there to see and come back to tell."

"Wouldn't it be a fascinating change," I said, "some year to plan a really different vacation? Pick some village lost on the plains where you don't know a soul and go there?"

"You'd be bored stiff."

Meet the Author
Ray Bradbury (1920–) is generally regarded as today's leading writer of fantasy and science fiction. He was born in Waukegan, Illinois, and at the age of twelve he was given a typewriter as a gift. Since then he has written more than a thousand short stories, many novels, and television, radio, and motion-picture scripts. His short-story collections include *The Illustrated Man* and *The Martian Chronicles*. *Fahrenheit 451* is his best-known novel.

"I'm not bored thinking of it!" I peered out the window. "What's the next town coming up on this line?"

"Rampart Junction."

I smiled. "Sounds good. I might get off there."

"You're a liar and a fool. What you want? Adventure? Romance? Go ahead, jump off the train. Ten seconds later you'll call yourself an idiot, grab a taxi, and race us to the next town."

"Maybe."

The train rounded a curve suddenly. I swayed. Far ahead I saw one church spire, a deep forest, a field of summer wheat.

"It looks like I'm getting off the train," I said.

"Sit down," he said.

"No," I said. "There's something about that town up ahead. I've got to go see. I've got the time. I don't have to be in L.A., really, until next Monday. If I don't get off the train now, I'll always wonder what I missed, what I let slip by when I had the chance to see it."

"We were just talking. There's nothing there."

"You're wrong," I said. "There is."

I put my hat on my head and lifted the suitcase in my hand.

"I think you're really going to do it," said the salesman.

My heart beat quickly. My face was flushed.

The train whistled. The train rushed down the track. The town was near!

"Wish me luck," I said.

"Luck!" he cried.

I ran for the porter, yelling.

There was an ancient, flake-painted chair tilted back against the station-platform wall. In this chair, completely relaxed so he sank into his clothes, was a man of some seventy years whose timbers looked as if he'd been nailed there since the station was built.

As I stepped down, the old man's eyes flicked every door on the train and stopped, surprised, at me.

I started up the dirt road toward the town. One hundred yards away, I glanced back.

The old man, still seated there, stared at the sun, as if posing a question.

I hurried on.

It was a town where nothing happened, where occurred only the following events:

At four o'clock sharp, the Honneger Hardware door slammed as a dog came out to dust himself in the road. Four-thirty, a straw sucked emptily at the bottom of a soda glass, making a sound like a great cataract[1] in the drugstore silence. Five o'clock, boys and pebbles plunged in the town river. Five-fifteen, ants paraded in the slanting light under some elm trees.

All through the afternoon there was only one constant and unchanging factor: the old man in the bleached blue pants and shirt was never far away. When I sat in the drugstore, he was out front spitting tobacco that rolled itself into tumblebugs in the dust. When I stood by the river, he was crouched downstream making a great thing of washing his hands.

Along about seven-thirty in the evening, I was walking for the seventh or eighth time through the quiet streets when I heard foot-steps beside me.

I looked over, and the old man was pacing me, looking straight ahead, a piece of dried grass in his stained teeth.

"It's been a long time," he said quietly. "A long time," he said, "waitin' on that station platform."

1. **cataract:** waterfall; a great rush of water.

"You?" I said

"Me." He nodded in the tree shadows.

"Were you waiting for someone at the station?"

"Yes," he said. "You."

"Me?" The surprise must have shown in my voice. "But why . . . ? You never saw me before in your life."

"Did I say I did? I just said I was waitin'."

"You want to know anything about me?" I asked suddenly. "You the sheriff?"

"No, not the sheriff. And no, I don't want to know nothing about you." He put his hands in his pockets. The sun was set now. The air was suddenly cool. "I'm just surprised you're here at last, is all."

"Surprised?"

"Surprised," he said, "and . . . pleased."

I stopped abruptly and looked straight at him.

"How long have you been sitting on that station platform?"

"Twenty years, give or take a few."

I knew he was telling the truth; his voice was as easy and quiet as the river.

"Waiting for me?" I said.

"Or someone like you," he said.

We walked on in the growing dark.

"How you like our town?"

"Nice, quiet," I said.

"Nice, quiet." He nodded. "Like the people?"

"People look nice and quiet."

"They are," he said, "Nice, quiet."

I was ready to turn back, but the old man kept talking; and in order to listen and be polite, I had to walk with him in the vaster darkness, the tides of field and meadow beyond town.

"Yes," said the old man, "the day I retired, twenty years ago, I sat down on that station platform, and there I been sittin', doin' nothin', waitin' for something to happen; I didn't know what, I didn't know, I couldn't say. But when it finally happened, I'd know it; I'd look at it and say, yes, sir, that's what I was waitin' for. Train wreck? No. Old woman friend come back to town after fifty years? No. No. It's hard to say. Someone. Something. And it seems to have something to do with you. I wish I could say—"

"Why don't you try?" I said.

"Well," he said slowly, "you know much about your own insides?"

"You mean my stomach, or you mean psychologically?"

"That's the word. I mean your head, your brain; you know much about *that*?"

"A little."

"You hate many people in your time?"

"Some."

"We all do. It's normal enough to hate, ain't it, and not only hate, but while we don't talk about it, don't we sometimes want to hit people who hurt us, even *kill* them?"

"Hardly a week passes we don't get that feeling," I said, "and put it away."

"Now," said the old man, looking at the water, "the only kind of killin' worth doin' is the one where nobody can guess who did it or why they did it or who they did it to, right? Well, I got this idea maybe twenty years ago. I don't think about it every day or every week. Sometimes months go by, but the idea's this: only one train stops here each day, sometimes not even that.

"Now, if you wanted to kill someone, you'd have to wait, wouldn't you, for years and years, until a complete and actual stranger came to your town, a stranger who got off the train for no reason, a man nobody knows, and who don't know nobody in the town. Then, and only then, I thought, sittin' there on the

129

station chair, you could just go up and when nobody's around, kill him and throw him in the river. He'd be found miles downstream. Maybe he'd never be found. Nobody would ever think to come to Rampart Junction to find him. He wasn't goin' there. He was on his way someplace else. There, that's my whole idea. And I'd know the man the minute he got off the train. Know him, just as clear . . ."

"Would you?" I said.

"Yes," he said. I saw the motion of his head looking at the stars. "Well, I've talked enough." He sidled[2] close and touched my elbow. His hand was feverish, as if he had held it to a stove before touching me. His other hand, his right hand, was hidden, tight and bunched, in his pocket. "I've talked enough."

The old man and I stood looking at each other in the dark. His left hand was still holding my elbow. His other hand was still hidden.

"May I say something?" I said at last.

The old man nodded.

"About myself," I said. I had to stop. I could hardly breathe. I forced myself to go on. "It's funny. I've often thought the same way as you. Sure, just today, going cross-country, I thought, how perfect, how really perfect it could be. Business has been bad for me

---
2. **sidled:** move sideways slowly.

lately. Wife sick. Good friend died last week. War in the world. Full of boils, myself. It would do me a world of good—"

"What?" the old man said, his hand on my arm.

"To get off this train in a small town," I said, "where nobody knows me, with this gun under my arm, and find someone and kill him and bury him and go back down to the station and get on and go home and nobody the wiser and nobody ever to know who did it, ever. Perfect, I thought, a perfect crime. And I got off the train."

"How do I know you got a gun under your arm?"

"You don't know." My voice blurred. "You can't be sure."

He waited. I thought he was going to faint.

"That's how it is?" he said.

"That's how it is," I said.

He shut his eyes tight. He shut his mouth tight.

After another five seconds, very slowly, heavily, he managed to take his hand away from my own immensely heavy arm. He looked down at his right hand then, and took it empty, out of his pocket.

Slowly, with great weight, we turned away from each other and started walking blind, completely blind, in the dark.

SELECTING DETAILS FROM THE STORY.
The following questions help you check your
reading comprehension. Put an *x* in the box
next to each correct answer.

1. The salesman decided to get off the
   train in
   ☐ a. Los Angeles.
   ☐ b. Rampart Junction.
   ☐ c. Chicago.

2. Sitting in a chair tilted against the
   platform wall was
   ☐ a. a man of about seventy.
   ☐ b. the sheriff.
   ☐ c. a very dangerous and menacing
        young fellow.

3. According to the old man, he had been
   waiting for someone like the salesman for
   ☐ a. several days.
   ☐ b. nearly a year.
   ☐ c. about twenty years.

4. The salesman said that he was carrying
   ☐ a. a briefcase.
   ☐ b. a gun.
   ☐ c. some samples.

KNOWING NEW VOCABULARY WORDS. The
following questions check your vocabulary
skills. Put an *x* in the box next to each correct
answer.

1. Far off in the distance he could see a
   church spire. Which of the following best
   defines the word *spire*?
   ☐ a. tower
   ☐ b. floor
   ☐ c. yard

2. The old man's eyes flicked over every
   door on the train, and then stopped at
   the stranger. What is the meaning of the
   word *flicked*?
   ☐ a. closed suddenly
   ☐ b. moved quickly
   ☐ c. ached painfully

3. "Psychologically?" asked the salesman.
   "That's the word," answered the old man.
   "I mean your head, your brain." Define
   the word *psychologically*.
   ☐ a. related to the mind
   ☐ b. related to the heart
   ☐ c. related to the skin

4. His hand was feverish "as if he had
   held it to a stove." As used here, the
   word *feverish* means
   ☐ a. stiff.
   ☐ b. trembling.
   ☐ c. very warm.

☐ × 5 = ☐

NUMBER   YOUR
CORRECT   SCORE

☐ × 5 = ☐

NUMBER   YOUR
CORRECT   SCORE

IDENTIFYING STORY ELEMENTS. The following questions check your knowledge of story elements. Put an *x* in the box next to each correct answer.

1. What is the *setting* of the story?
   - ☐ a. a quiet country town
   - ☐ b. a large and busy community
   - ☐ c. a small city

2. What happened last in the *plot* of the story?
   - ☐ a. The salesman wandered around, then stopped in the drugstore for a soda.
   - ☐ b. The two men walked slowly away from each other.
   - ☐ c. The old man revealed his plan to the salesman.

3. Identify the old man's *motive* for waiting for a stranger.
   - ☐ a. to rob him
   - ☐ b. to kill him
   - ☐ c. to ask his advice

4. Which expression best describes the *mood* of the selection?
   - ☐ a. joyous and cheerful
   - ☐ b. light and amusing
   - ☐ c. strange and mysterious

LOOKING AT CLOZE. The following questions use the cloze technique to check your reading comprehension. Complete the paragraph by filling in each blank with one of the words listed below. Each word appears in the story. Since there are five words and four blanks, one of the words will not be used.

Many people find building model railroads a _____ hobby. Locomotives, cars, and _____ are generally purchased in kits and must be assembled, piece by piece, with painstaking care. The miniature parts are constructed *to scale*— that is, in exact proportion to the parts on the _____ railroad. Hobbyists say they are willing to invest the time, effort, and money required because building model railroads is _____ enjoyable.

immensely   actual

fascinating

trains   peered

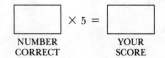

NUMBER CORRECT   × 5 =   YOUR SCORE

NUMBER CORRECT   × 5 =   YOUR SCORE

LEARNING HOW TO READ CRITICALLY.
The following questions check your critical thinking skills. Put an *x* in the box next to each correct answer.

1. Clues in the story indicate that after the salesman arrived, the old man
   ☐ a. spent most of the day following him.
   ☐ b. went home until the evening when he left to find him.
   ☐ c. remained at the station for several hours.

2. The old man's "other hand, his right hand, was hidden, tight and bunched, in his pocket." This is the author's way of suggesting that the old man
   ☐ a. felt chilled from the cold.
   ☐ b. was carrying a great deal of money.
   ☐ c. was carrying a gun.

3. At the conclusion of the story, the salesman probably felt
   ☐ a. pleased that he had decided to visit.
   ☐ b. anxious to spend more time in the town.
   ☐ c. very relieved and eager to leave.

4. We may infer that the old man was
   ☐ a. popular.
   ☐ b. crazy.
   ☐ c. happy.

Improving Writing and Discussion Skills

- Did the salesman really have a gun— or was he bluffing? Give reasons for your answer.
- The salesman walked along with the old man until they found themselves in a deserted place in the vast darkness of field and meadow. Why do you think the old man took that route? Why did the salesman go along with him?
- Suppose you were the salesman. Describe to a friend your encounter with the old man. Tell what went through your mind and how you felt and acted.

Use the boxes below to total your scores for the exercises. Then write your score on pages 135 and 136.

☐ **S**ELECTING DETAILS FROM THE STORY
+
☐ **K**NOWING NEW VOCABULARY WORDS
+
☐ **I**DENTIFYING STORY ELEMENTS
+
☐ **L**OOKING AT CLOZE
+
☐ **L**EARNING HOW TO READ CRITICALLY
▼
☐ **S**core Total: Story 15

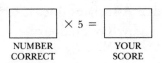

☐ × 5 = ☐

NUMBER   YOUR
CORRECT   SCORE

Acknowledgments

Acknowledgment is gratefully made to the following publishers, authors, and agents for permission to reprint these works. Every effort has been made to determine copyright owners. In the case of any omissions, the Publisher will be pleased to make suitable acknowledgments in future editions.

"The Wise and the Weak" by Philip Aponte. Reprinted by permission of Scholastic Inc. from *Literary Cavalcade*, 1954. ©1954 by Scholastic Inc.

"Dear Marsha" by Judie Angell. ©1989 by Judie Angell from *Connections: Short Stories* by Donald R. Gallo, Editor. Used by permission of Delacorte Press, a division of Bantam Doubleday Dell Publishing Group, Inc.

"Polar Night" by Norah Burke. From *Story* by Norah Burke. Used by permission of Scholastic Inc.

"I'll Give You Law" by Molly Picon. All attempts have been made to contact the copyright holder.

"A Habit for the Voyage" by Robert Edmond Alter. From *Hitchcock* magazine, September 1964. Copyright renewed 1992. Used by permission of the Larry Sternig Literary Agency.

"Eleven" by Sandra Cisneros. From *Women Hollering Creek*. ©1991 by Sandra Cisneros. Published in the United States by Vintage Books, a division of Random House, Inc., New York. Originally published in hardcover by Random House, Inc. in 1991. Reprinted by permission of the Susan Bergholz Literary Services, New York.

"The Clearing" by Jesse Stuart. Copyright by Jesse Stuart and the Jesse Stuart Foundation. Adapted by permission of the Jesse Stuart Foundation, P.O. Box 391, Ashland, Kentucky 41114.

"The Medicine Bag" by Virginia Driving Hawk Sneve. Reprinted by permission of Virginia Driving Hawk Sneve and *Boys' Life* magazine, published by the Boy Scouts of America.

"The Fun They Had" by Isaac Asimov. Published by permission of the Estate of Isaac Asimov, c/o Ralph M. Vicinanza, Ltd.

"Lonesome Boy" by Arna Bontemps. ©1955 by Arna Bontemps and Feliks Topolski. © renewed 1983 by Mrs. Arna (Alberta) Bontemps and Feliks Topolski. Reprinted by permission of Houghton Mifflin Co. All rights reserved.

"My Father Goes to Court" by Carlos Bulosan. Excerpts from "My Father Goes to Court" in *The Laughter of My Father* by Carlos Bulosan, ©1944 by Harcourt Brace & Company, reprinted by permission of the publisher.

"The Town Where No One Got Off" by Ray Bradbury. Reprinted by permission of Don Congdon Associates, Inc. ©1958, renewed 1986 by Ray Bradbury.

Progress Chart

1. Write in your score for each exercise.
2. Write in your Score Total.

	S	K	I	L	L	SCORE TOTAL
Story 1						
Story 2						
Story 3						
Story 4						
Story 5						
Story 6						
Story 7						
Story 8						
Story 9						
Story 10						
Story 11						
Story 12						
Story 13						
Story 14						
Story 15						

Progress Graph

1. Write your Score Total in the box under the number for each story.
2. Put an *x* along the line above each box to show your Score Total for that story.
3. Make a graph of your progress by drawing a line to connect the *x*'s.

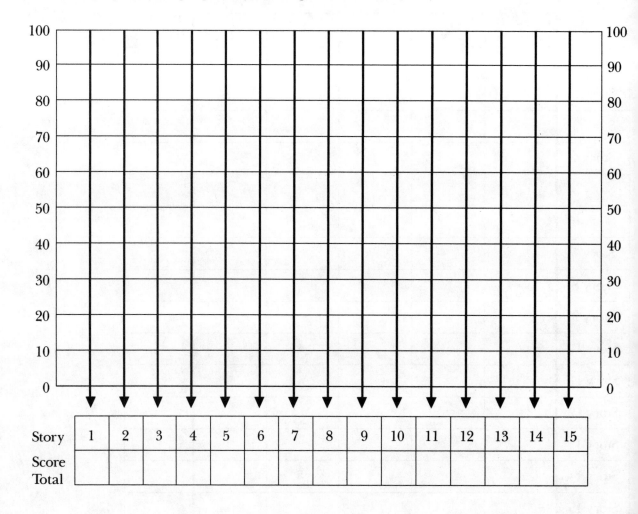

Story	1	2	3	4	5	6	7	8	9	10	11	12	13	14	15
Score Total